# UNCREATED ENERGY

# UNCREATED ENERGY

## A Journey into the Authentic Sources of Christian Faith

GEORGE MALONEY

AMITY HOUSE
AMITY, NEW YORK

Published by Amity House Inc.
106 Newport Bridge Road
Warwick, NY 10990



Revised edition of *A Theology of Uncreated Energies,* Marguette University Press, Milwaukee, Wis., 1978.



Library of Congress Card Catalog Number 87-81807

ISBN 0-916349-20-9

ACKNOWLEDGMENT

I am grateful to Sister Joseph Agnes of the Sisters of Charity of Halifax for her kindness in reading and typing this manuscript.

## DEDICATION

To My Fellow Jesuit Brothers
of the Wisconsin Province

# Contents

Introduction . . . . . . . . . . . . . . . . . . . . . . . . . . . . . . 1

*CHAPTER ONE*

Invaded by God . . . . . . . . . . . . . . . . . . . . . . . . . . . . . 5

*CHAPTER TWO*

In Search of a Process . . . . . . . . . . . . . . . . . . . . . . . . 27

*CHAPTER THREE*

Knowing the Unknowable God . . . . . . . . . . . . . . . . 41

*CHAPTER FOUR*

The Uncreated Energies . . . . . . . . . . . . . . . . . . . . . 59

*CHAPTER FIVE*

Theological Applications of Divine Energies . . . . . . . 81

Notes . . . . . . . . . . . . . . . . . . . . . . . . . . . . . . . . . . . 97

# Introduction

What we are noticing in the West, especially in theology, is the breakdown of Western Christendom's cultural dominance. This can be a breakthrough to a new era of exciting theologizing that frees us in the West from certain outmoded cultural forms that hold back persons from encountering the "living God of Abraham, Isaac and Jacob." Static forms have stood too long in the way of true theology as a medium, a science to bring people into an experience of the transcendent-immanent God.

Karl Jaspers in his work, *The Origin and Goal of History*, speaks of the great transitions in the history of humanity: 1. the *axial* transition of the "first millenium" when genuine personal consciousness as we know it today emerged; 2. our present rationalistic and technological age, which both threatens the destruction of the axial breakthrough by restricting human consciousness to only one of its capacities and simultaneously promises a heightened awareness of human personhood; 3. the future planetization of humanity, which both promises a further expansion of human consciousness beyond cultural boundaries and demands it, for as the world becomes increasingly one, what happens now becomes absolutely decisive.[1]

William M. Thompson builds on Jasper's thesis to maintain that Christians are entering into an individuation process, made "possible in direct proportion to, not in inverse proportion to, one's awareness of God and affirmation of the resurrection belief."[2]

Such an understanding of one's own unique *I-ness* comes most intensely in a love experience of God in prayer. For in Teilhard de Chardin's words: "Love differentiates as it unites." As we move into the dialectical tension between the experience of God in His awesome *Otherness*, in His transcendence, beyond us and outside of us, and the experience of God intimately present to us in His indwelling immanence, theology opens up an exciting dialogue in communion between God and man.

It is my thesis that in the history of Christianity there were theologians, especially among the illustrious Greek Fathers who formulated for us the great pivotal Christian doctrines of the Trinity, Christology, grace, redemption and the mystery of the Church as prophetic sign of Christ's risen presence still among us, who reached such a stage of individuation by experiencing a living theology of the Risen Savior. These were theologians who were individuated mystics. They theologized from their experience of God in His scriptural Word.

They developed a positive, speculative theology *(cataphatic)*. But they put this always in the context of *apophatic* mystery. This *apophaticism* was not a mere negation of man's intellectual powers to explore the awesome transcendence of God. It was a call to worship and receive God's revelation in a prayerful mystery that was a positive knowledge of God given by God's Holy Spirit to the pure of heart.

What was available to an elite group of theologians is today being made available to all Christians, regardless of any limiting cultural factors. This book is an attempt to gather something of the dynamic vision of the Greek Fathers into a presentation, using the model of God's *uncreated energies* as distinct from God's eternal essence. By investigating the thought of such Greek Fathers, especially by using the final synthesis made by St. Gregory Palamas (+1359), we can break free of a staticism in our Western theology and still avoid the failures of the modern process theologians who fail to present a dialectic that preserves in antinomy both the transcendence and immanence of God.

A modest appeal will be made to reconcile speculative theology with mystical theology and thus heal the wounds of medieval theology that looked upon theology so often as solely a speculative science, but lost the corrective to true theology that only an authentic mysticism could restore.

George A. Maloney, S.J.
Contemplative Ministries
Midway City, CA

*CHAPTER ONE*

# Invaded by God

Batter my heart, three-personed God; for You
as yet but knock, breathe, shine and seek to mend;
That I may rise, and stand, o'erthrow me, and bend
Your force, to break, blow, burn and make me new.
I, like an usurped town, to another due,
Labor to admit You, but oh! to no end;
Reason, Your viceroy in me, me should defend,
But is captived and proves weak or untrue.
Yet dearly I love You, and would be loved fain,
But am betrothed to Your enemy.
Divorce me, untie, or break that knot again,
Take me to you, imprison me, for I
except You enthrall me, never shall be free;
Nor even chaste, except you ravish me.

John Donne

Only if God ravish us shall we be what God created us to be. In the words of St. Irenaeus of the second century, we are empty receptacles to be filled by God. God first freely creates us; then freely He seeks to communicate Himself to us as intellectual beings capable of hearing His Word. All this is in order that He may share His very trinitarian life with us.

Yet how we poor human beings will do just about anything to avoid surrendering to God's pervading loving presence! We fear to enter into God's burning love, because, if we do, we know we must *die.* We must allow His consuming love to destroy all vestige of self-centeredness. He alone must become God for us. We must live only for Him and in Him alone we shall find our true being.

But before that surrender to God's supremacy over us, what an agony of resistance we put up. Nikos Kazantzakis describes it: "God is fire and you must walk on it. . . dance on it. At that moment the fire will become cool water. But until you reach that point, what a struggle, my Lord, what agony!"

## LORD, THAT I MAY SEE!

We were meant, as Adam and Eve before the fall, to walk through this world and commune with God. We should be able to see God in the rain drop, in the soft colors of the evening sunset, in the thunder and lightning, in snow and frost, in heat and cold. But we do not. We are not in touch with God's energetic love that assumes millions of concrete manifestations surrounding us at every moment, even though He is touching us with His millions of fingers.

The poet and the mystic can still see Him. Gerard Manley Hopkins saw the world as "charged with the grandeur of God. It will flame out, like shining from shook foil . . ." Yet man through greedy commerce has bleared his eyes and fails to see this grandeur. Still it is there.

And for all this, nature is never spent;
There lives the dearest freshness deep down things;
And though the last lights off the black West went
Oh, morning, at the brown brink eastward, springs—
Because the Holy Ghost over the bent
World broods with warm breast and with ah! bright wings.[1]

God in His infinite love breaks out of His trinitarian *We*-community to want to share His life with us human beings. We tremble before the awesome holiness, yes, His very humility that must be at the heart of such a free love in our regard.

## A GRACEFUL LOVE

Love, in order to exist, in man or God, must always be loving, always pouring itself out from its own abundance, always giving of itself. Tied to the mysterious makeup of God as an *I* that is also a *We*, is God's bursting forth from within His own perfect, circular, loving, self-containment to love us so that we might accept His love and become happy in sharing His own very family-life, that of the Trinity. The nature of God is such that, while being one in essence, it demands a plurality as objects of His love, of His infinite Self-giving. Love is the best word that St. John and any other human being could choose to describe God's relations to man.

God spills out His love in activity in the creation of human beings and the universe, in the Incarnation of His Divine Son, Jesus Christ, in the Redemption by the God-Man of the whole human and subhuman cosmos, in the sanctification and final Parousia through the Holy Spirit. These are all actions of God prompted by the one constant act of love.

St. Irenaeus pictures God as coming toward us in the

created world through His two hands, Jesus Christ and the Holy Spirit.

> And therefore throughout all time, man, having been moulded at the beginning by the hands of God, that is, of the Son and the Spirit, is made after the image and likeness of God.[2]

The Greek Fathers carefully distinguish between the essence of God that is one nature, equally shared by the three Divine Persons, and God's one nature in the multiplied world of creation. Pseudo-Dionysius describes the movement outwardly toward the created world as a "going forth" of God (*proodos* in Greek). The importance of this distinction is rooted in God's revelation. His essence no human being can see or comprehend in any human fashion. No man has ever seen God and lived (Ex 33:23; 1 Jn 4:12; Jn 1:18; 6:46).

Yet God lovingly wishes to share His very own being with us. In man's very own creation, as described in *Genesis*, the trinitarian We-community freely decides to make man in a way that he could share in God's life. "Let us make man in our own image, in the likeness of ourselves" (Gn 1:26). God only asks that man open himself to God's many "goings-forth" in which God wishes to communicate His great, personal love for man. In man's constant response to this invitation of God's love consists all his greatness and fulfillment. If he consents by humbling himself to his true ontological place as a creature before his Creator, if he makes himself supple and malleable in the hands of the Divine Artist, God can make of him His chef-d'oeuvre, a true, loving child of God in union with the only Begotten Son, Jesus Christ, co-heir with Him of Heaven forever. It is man's loving in return (always made possible through God's energizing grace) that divinizes us, brings us into a oneness in love so that God truly lives in us by participation.

"God is love and anyone who lives in love lives in God and God lives in him" (1 Jn 4:16). Grace, therefore, is God loving His human creation and deifying it through His activity with human beings who freely choose the Way to the Truth that leads to Life which is Love Personified.

Through the doctrine of God's energies of love, the Trinity as one in essence but now conceived of as "God for us," we can solve the antinomy between a God who cannot in any way be comprehended in His essence and a God who is constantly communicating Himself to us through creation. The end of the created order, as seen by the early Fathers in their theologizing from Holy Scripture, is that God might divinize us through sharing His trinitarian life. This means that we are capable not only of communicating with God in true knowledge but also entering into a loving communion with Him. The experiencing of the divine energies, God the Father, Son and Holy Spirit, acting as one God, makes it possible for us to enter into a mystical union with God.

## GOD'S ENERGIES

God gives Himself to us through His loving actions. But the importance of understanding the doctrine of God's energies is that His actions are not *things* God does to us or on our behalf. God's energetic actions are God as He, from His one essence, gives Himself to us dynamically. This is *primarily* what grace is for the Greek Fathers.

Such a distinction presents God as always dynamically giving Himself to us in order that we might have a share in His "uncreated" nature as 2 P 1:4 holds out as the aim of our life. It avoids any static, objectivizing of grace as primarily a created accident that man can live without. St. Thomas Aquinas, using Aristotle's categories, defines grace as the external principle of human actions. "Man needs a power added to his natural power by grace," wrote St. Thomas.[3]

What is crucial in this doctrine is that through God's energies we actually do make contact with the living God. God is truly love. He must, therefore, want to give us, not merely a created grace, but Himself as Gift. The energies are really God and not a created thing. God does give us Himself directly as He is personalized in His energies.

## APPROPRIATION

We come down to the important and crucial point of this book. If God is a loving *We* community, does He really give Himself to us in a personalized way? If Holy Scripture and the Tradition of the Church present God as Father, Son and Holy Spirit, a community of oneness in inter-relationships of a we, then are we capable of entering into such personal relationships with the Trinity? Does God only give us Himself, not as He truly is, but through means of a gift, called created grace? Or does He allow us to know and love Him in relationships of Father, Son and Spirit?

First, we need to understand the term used by theologians from St. Augustine's time, namely, *appropriations.* It refers to our assigning a certain power or quality to one of the three Divine Persons, even though, as we have just said, any action of God is of God's essential energy of love and is common to all three Persons. However, because of a similarity between that given quality and the distinct, personalized relationship within the Trinity certain attributes were assigned by theologians and spiritual writers to individual Persons. Thus power was associated with the Father since He is the Source of the processions of the Son and Holy Spirit. Wisdom was assigned to the Son since He proceeds as the Word and Image of the Father. Goodness was associated with the Holy Spirit since He is the fullness and loving completion of the Trinity and God's Gift to us in whom all gifts are given.[4]

The language of appropriation allows us to discuss the essential divine attributes of the Trinity as found reflected in creation. It also allows us to find reflections of the Trinity in the beliefs of other religions such as Hinduism and Buddhism.[5] But what is important to remember is that such attributes flow from the total, divine essence and are not "personalized" qualities predicated solely to any one of the Persons of the Trinity. To understand what is personal and proper to each member, as St. Bonaventure wrote, Christian faith is required.[6]

In terms of Byzantine theology all actions that flow from the divine energies are common to all Persons. From our viewpoint, the manifestations of these energies are multiple. From that of the Trinity, there is one, divine energy attributable to the divine essence, therefore, to the common action of all three Persons. St. Gregory Palamas uses the example of the one sun giving off a ray that equally gives warmth, light, life and nourishment.[7]

## A COSMIC TRANSFIGURATION

God is not only continually revealing Himself as Love through His manifold energies flowing from the one essence of God, shared equally by all three Persons in the Trinity, but God is also involved within that revelation of Himself as Love to transfigure this universe into a divinized whole, into the Cosmic Christ.[8] Not only human beings but the whole human cosmos is under "the bondage of corruption" (Rm 8:21) and we daily experience that the whole creation groans and travails in pain together (Rm 8:22).

But we also believe that God truly loves the world He

created. "And God saw that it was good!" (Gn 1:18). He has created all things, every atom of matter, in and through His Word, Jesus Christ. God is present inside of all that exists. "For in him we live and move and have our being" (Ac 17:28). These energies of God bathe the whole universe and charge it with His infinite love. Although at times, all around us may seem to be in chaotic confusion and life has "no exit," as Sartre gave as the final judgement of the world, nevertheless, we Christians must be able to touch God in His energies as He reveals Himself to us in these material manifestations. Above all, we must be able to be touched and transformed into godly creatures by grace.

God is not only transcendent, but by His energies He becomes immanently present throughout all of creation. God as love seeks to become more "present" to us through every creature that He gives us. We can say that God becomes truly transcendent, standing infinitely above, apart, outside of the created, finite world precisely because His infinite energies, uncreated acts of love, flowing out from His essence as God, penetrate immanently the whole created world. His energies touch the core of each being and exert a loving attraction to draw all things unto Himself. We human beings especially are being drawn constantly into the very heart of God in order to be divinized and to share the triune life. In God's transcendence and immanence, the dynamism of His energies is an interaction with us human beings, all in order to lead us to a transfiguration whereby we will be truly made sharers in the very life and love of the Holy Trinity.

## GOD'S SELF-REVELATION

Michael Schmaus points out that God reveals Himself to us on a vertical and also a horizontal plane. On the vertical level God reveals Himself to us through the created nature and human spirits, that is, we can know God through His presence in creatures of nature but also through His presence operating in our intellectual faculties. He also reveals Himself on this level through Christ, namely, the Divine Word, that becomes flesh and dwells among us (Jn 1:14). God also reveals Himself within the context of our horizontal, historical existence through the creation of the world, the revelation of Jesus Christ, the Incarnate Word, and in the fulfillment of the world.[9]

These two levels cross each other and it is in their inter-relationships of these levels that we come to the "economic" relationships of God, both in His energies, commonly shared by all three Divine Persons, and in the personalized relationships of each Person to the created world. It is precisely in the person of Jesus Christ that we find the Way to enter into this mystery of God's invasion of us and the whole created world, not only by His uncreated energies of love but by the unique actions of each Person of the Trinity continuing in an analogous way the basic "immanent" and personalized acts that constitute each Person His unique Self.

We would always have believed that God would touch us and communicate Himself to us only through the energies. We would always have been unable to enter into "personalized" relationships with the Father, different from those of the Son and the Holy Spirit, if it had not been for the Incarnation. For this mystery of the Incarnation reveals to us through the materiality of the human nature of Christ what our own humanity can attain by grace. This dogma of the hypostatic union teaches us that the Second Person of the Trinity who operates equally and conjointly with the other two Persons in all "energetic" actions throughout the universe, acted in the historical horizontal level in a unique manner that reflected somewhat His very own oppositional relationships to the Father and the Holy Spirit within the immanent life of the Trinity. The Person of the Word of God, different from the Father and the Spirit, but not separated, assumed a human nature. This nature did not exist of itself and then was merely added somehow to the Divine Word. In that very act the Word gave existence to His human nature and divinized it.

This humanity had the immortal and incorruptible character of the nature of Adam before he sinned, yet Jesus Christ in that humanity was subjected to the conditions of our own fallen natures, as St. Maximus the Confessor writes.[10] Christ is the *Pontifex Maximus*, the greatest of all bridge-builders, who spans the infinite world of God (including the personalized world of the three Persons) and the finite world of mankind and created beings. St. Maximus writes:

> We are astonished to see how the finite and the infinite—things which exclude one another and cannot be mixed—are found to be united in Him and are manifested mutually the one in the other. For the unlimited is limited in an ineffable manner, while the limited is stretched to the measure of the unlimited.[11]

The Second Person as Logos has been revealing the hidden Godhead from the beginning of creation with a personalized act different from the Father. The Father and Source of all being creates all the created world in and through His Word by the overshadowing of His Spirit of love. "Through him all things came to be, not one thing had its being but through him. All that came to be had life in him . . ." (Jn 1:1-2). The Word, within the "conactual," one, energetic manifestation of God, exerts His own proper, personalistic action. This, Scripture reveals to us as a specific act of imaging the Father through knowledge discovered throughout all nature and within the intellectual powers of man himself.

But through the Incarnation the Second Person continues now through the humanity assumed by the Logos to reveal Himself to us through specific actions reflecting that immanent action of the Son within the Trinity. The human nature of Christ is totally penetrated by the one, divine nature, yet it always remains distinct from that divine nature. It is "existentially" united to the Second Person of the Trinity and not to the First, the Father, nor to the Third, the Holy Spirit.

## THEOSIS–DIVINIZATION

St. Athanasius succinctly summarizes the end of the Incarnation:

> The Divine Word was made man that we might become gods. He was made visible through His body in order that we might have an idea of the invisible Father. He has supported the outrages of men in order that we may have a part of His immortality.[12]

As the Heavenly Father eternally begets His Son, so in the "economic" order in history, in the life of Jesus Christ and in a parallel way in our own lives, that same Father is begetting His Son, Jesus Christ, and through Him and His Holy Spirit, He is begetting us in His Son to be His adopted children. St. Cyril of Alexandria writes:

> By the Incarnation we also in Him and through Him according to nature and grace have been made sons of God. According to nature insofar as we are one in Him (through the same human nature); by participation and according to grace through Himself in the Spirit.[13]

The end of our lives is to grow continually into an ever increasing awareness of oneness in Christ Jesus. This is what the Greek Fathers mean by *divinization.* We are to live in the "likeness" of Jesus Christ, that is, to share in His very own life made possible by the Holy Spirit. St. Bernard preached that God entices us to love Him by giving us the humanity of His Son as the point of attraction. Jesus Christ images the divinity of God that radiates through the frailness and lowliness of His humanity. His meekness and gentleness draw us without any threatening fear to surrender to His Spirit. The glory or power of God in His Word radiates in the teachings and miracles and healings of Jesus in Scripture.

It is through this man, Jesus of Nazareth, who will die

and be raised up from the dead, that all of God's grace and glory will come to us.

> Indeed, from his fullness we have, all of us, received—
> yes, grace in return for grace,
> since, though the Law was given through Moses,
> grace and truth have come through Jesus Christ.
> No one has ever seen God;
> it is the only Son, who is nearest to the Father's heart,
> who has made him known (Jn 1:16-18)

Jesus Christ perfectly and faithfully represents His Father to us in human communication of words and actions. When He loves us, especially by dying for us on the Cross, we can experience the love of the Father. "As the Father has loved me, so I have loved you" (Jn 15:9). Everything He says or does is *the* Word of God. He can do nothing but what the Father tells Him to do. Yet only Jesus Christ, the Second Person of the Trinity in His human nature, goes to His death. It is not the Father who dies for us nor the Holy Spirit. Yet all three Persons are involved in the Incarnation and Redemption, in our sanctification, each according to His own personalized acts. The Father begets His Son through the overshadowing of the Spirit, as St. Luke records in Lk 1:35. The Father continues acting His personalized role as Begetter in our own divinization through His Son and the Holy Spirit.

## THE ROLE OF THE HOLY SPIRIT

The goal of our human existence is to be divinized through the personalized actions of the Father, Son and Holy Spirit into a likeness to the Son of God in the Holy Spirit. It is a process of becoming as God is: a We-community that is personalized Love in a oneness of nature and in uniqueness of persons. As both the Son and the Holy Spirit "proceed" from the Father as from their Source, so they cannot be separated in their "economic" actions that, nevertheless, are distinctive to each Person.

Because the Spirit is "hypostasized" Love binding the Father and Son together, some modern Orthodox theologians like to describe the work of the Holy Spirit in terms of a *kenosis* or emptying, a self-giving, the characteristic of personalized love. St. Paul describes the condescension of God's Word in taking upon Himself the form of a servant and emptying Himself by becoming obedient unto the death of the cross (Ph 2:5-8). That action of Jesus Christ who now is in glory goes on, due to the humanity that links Him with all of us human beings. But the *kenosis* of the Holy Spirit is a constant, hidden giving of the Father and Son to us that persists from Pentecost until the Parousia in this economy of salvation.[14]

The personality of the Holy Spirit is hidden in a personalized *Humility* that characterizes Love itself. He is personified Holiness because He reflects the essence of divine holiness.[15] The holiness of God is seen as triune Love in the Holy Spirit that S. Bulgakov calls: "hypostatic Love."[16]

The Holy Spirit is both the Giver and the Gift of life (Jn 6:63). He gives divine life to us through Jesus Christ but He is also the Father's Gift to us through Jesus Christ. All we have to do is to ask for this Gift and the Father will give us a share in Him (Lk 11:13). Jesus tells us also that Spirit is the "Parakletos" (Jn 16:24), who also gives us righteousness and peace (Rm 14:17). And above all He gives us love that makes it possible for us to be united in filiation with the Father (Jn 15:9; 17:26; Rm 5:5; Rm 8:15, Ga 4:6). The Spirit ushers us into the Kingdom of God. To seek the Kingdom of God is to seek the Holy Spirit for He pours into our hearts all the gifts necessary, not only to enter into living relationship with the Father and Jesus Christ, but also to build up the Kingdom of God.

The personality and work of the Holy Spirit can be seen only in the light of the personality and work of the Father and the Son. The Spirit is present in the eternal birth of the

Son. So also He realizes the conception of the Son in history in the womb of Mary. So also the Spirit effects our own being begotten of the Father through the Son. As Jesus in His lifetime was submissive to the Spirit and all of His acts—miracles, healings, forgiving of sins, driving out devils, especially the surrender of His very own life into the hands of His Heavenly Father—were performed by the action of the Spirit within the heart of Jesus Christ, so we find our fullness as human beings by being submissive to the Holy Spirit. The work of Jesus and the Spirit in the Incarnation and Redemption and in Pentecost through the Church of Jesus Christ is climaxed in the goal of the mutual cooperation of Jesus Christ and the Spirit to divinize us into children of the Heavenly Father. Neither Person is more important nor does one do more than the other. They "co-serve" each other to "recapitulate" or bring to completion the Father's eternal plan of creating us and sharing His life through His Son incarnate through the Spirit of Love.

As the Spirit brings the Father and Son together into a loving community and brings about in that mutual love a union of love and a self-knowledge in self-giving to each other, so the same Spirit brings us, many brothers and sisters, into the one begotten Son, Jesus Christ and constitutes the Body of Christ, the Church. Thomas Hopko shows the completing work of the Holy Spirit:

> Just as the work of Christ would be devoid of power without the 'power from on high' in a Pascha without a Pentecost, so would the Way remain unwalkable, the Truth unknowable and the Life unlivable. The Spirit comes to make possible in men all that Christ is by nature by the gracious gift of his presence. This is what St. Maximus means when he says that men are called to be by grace all that Christ is by nature. And what St. Basil means when he announces so boldly that men are 'creatures who have received a command to be god.'[17]

The role of the Spirit is especially "personalized" in our relationships to God as we see that He is not only the hidden person that is in the intimate relationships between Father and Son, but He also is the one who brings to the Father and the Son their unique knowledge and love of themselves and of each other precisely as persons. We come into our unique identity as persons, loved infinitely by the Father and His Son, Jesus, through the working of the Spirit that indwells us as in a temple (1 Co 3:16). We do not know how to pray, but the Spirit comes to our rescue and the Father knows what He is saying within us (Rm 8:26-27).

The greatest work of the Spirit is to unite us with God and as we are united with Him, especially in the personalistic relationships of the three Persons, we are capable of exercising His gifts, particularly the greatest, the gift of love and entering into a unity in the Body of Christ. Such a sense of oneness between ourselves and God and at the same time with every other living creature is the work of the Holy Spirit who infuses into us the gift of contemplation where prayer becomes love. Teilhard de Chardin beautifully expresses this:

> Reality is charged with a divine Presence. As the mystics sense and portray it, everything becomes physically and literally lovable in God; and reciprocally God becomes knowable and lovable in all that surrounds us. In the greatness and depths of its cosmic stuff in the maddening number of elements and events which compose it, and in the fullness of the general currents which dominate and set it in motion like a great wave, the World, filled with God, no longer appears to our opened eyes as anything but a milieu and an object of universal communion.[18]

## GOD IN ALL

Such a contemplative person lives in the dynamic creative presence of God in all things. He may start with a sunset or a small flower. He finds that God is there totally. He no longer feels the need to run frantically throughout the wonders of this world or to exhaust the gamut of human experiences in order to find God. This was perhaps more necessary in the beginning of his prayer life. As persons become more and more advanced in contemplation, especially by the loving presence of the Holy Spirit unifying all things in Christ who leads us to the Heavenly Father, they easily intuit God in all things. Touching anything created yields to them the loving presence of God at the core of all reality.

The dichotomy between the sacred and the secular worlds breaks down as does the separation between work and prayer. Whatever such a person is doing, he finds the Divine Presence everywhere in the unity of all things and this forces him out of himself in a spirit of worship and service. We are touching here ultimately the essential in celibacy. It is not so much physical, although in some chosen callings it includes this witness also. But theologically as experienced celibacy, it is the gift of the Holy Spirit to one who is now totally open to the presence of God and in love with the whole world because he has already participated in an experience of "seeing" God in all things and all things in God. Such a person cannot for a moment love another human being for himself alone. Yet he does not love that person only as a *means* to God. His love is a total grasp of the unique person and the unique presence of God that yields at the same time the unique presence of the personalized acts constituting each Divine Person as Father, Son and Holy Spirit.

We learn to experience God at the heart of all matter.[19] We love each being, this thing, this person, this tree, and God at the same time. We no longer have to move from this to God but we see at one and the same time the created being and the infinite love of God who creates this being and gives it to us as a gift of His love. We find the gift and the Giver in the same look.

Julian of Norwich expresses this well in her pondering of God in a little thing no bigger than a hazelnut that she holds in her hand.

> I looked at it with the eye of my understanding and thought: What can this be? I was amazed that it could last, for I thought that because of its littleness it would suddenly have fallen into nothing. And I was answered in my understanding: It lasts and always will, because God loves it; and thus everything has being through the love of God. . . It is that God is the Creator and the protector and the lover. For until I am substantially united to him, I can never have perfect rest or true happiness, until, that is, I am so attached to him that there can be no created thing between my God and me?[20]

## GOD WITHIN US

The progress in contemplation is to move more intimately toward God as the core of all reality, but this core is a bundle of infinite, unconfining Love. And as we grow in greater union with God, we begin to live in the power of that burning love that surrounds us in all things and permeates the depths of our being. Prayer moves away from a *doing*, above all, a speaking to God as to an object, to become a constant state of *being* in His love.

When Jesus spoke about prayer He used in His native Aramaic language the word *zlotha*, coming from the root word *zla*, as Dr. Rocco A. Errico explains?[21] This word means literally to "set a trap." In its modern use it would refer to focus in, to tune in to another's communication. Prayer for Jesus was adjusting His whole being to the presence of God living within His humanity. It was surrendering in His human consciousness to the trinitarian God, the Father, Son and Holy Spirit, living within Him and all about Him. Prayer was for Jesus to be receptive to God's personalized love actions at every moment. He surrendered to that love and became Godly-love toward all who met Him.

As Jesus grew in wisdom and knowledge and grace before God and men (Lk 2:52), He entered into a fuller awareness of God's perfect love and self-giving. For us contemplation is a growth through the infusion of faith, hope and love by the Spirit of Jesus Christ in awareness that God is always present loving us intimately and infinitely. How our attitude toward prayer changes when we see it as a listening and a receiving of God's communicating love for us, always constant, never changing!

God cannot increase His love for us, for in Christ Jesus has He not given us the fullness of His love? Can the indwelling Trinity be only imperfectly present in you? Does God wait for you to tell Him that you love Him and then He will come to you with a greater love? Does God's love for us become more ardent and perfect after we have performed for Him some good work? No, prayer is not our attempt to change God so that He will love us more. It is our "tuning in" to God's all-pervasive presence as perfect love. It is to find Him in all things as the power that creates and sustains creatures in being (Ac 17:28).

Above all, it is to live interiorly in the light of the trinitarian indwelling within us. We have seen that this "good news" of the triune God living within us can come to us only through God's revelation, known in Holy Scripture and in the Church that has received the knowledge and understanding to teach us prophetically with the mind of God. Through the mysteries of the Incarnation, death and resurrection of the Word-made-flesh, and His giving to us a constant release of the Spirit of love, we can believe with certainty that, as we die to sin or self-love, we open ourselves up more and more to the eternal, trinitarian community of love within us and around us.

As we die to our self-absorption and open to God's loving presence within us, God's gift of contemplation brings us a new way of knowing God and of receiving His eternal love for one another. Louis de Blois expresses this new level of living in God's indwelling love:

> The soul, having entered the vast solitude of the Godhead, happily loses itself; and enlightened by the brightness of most lucid darkness, becomes through knowledge as if without knowledge, and dwells in a sort of wise ignorance. And although it knows not what God is, to whom it is united by pure charity, although it sees not God as He is in His glory, it yet learns by experience that He infinitely transcends all sensible things, and all that can be apprehended by the human intellect concerning Him. It knows God by this intimate embrace and contact better than the eyes of the body know the visible sun. This soul well knows what true contemplation is.[22]

## GOD WITHIN AND WITHOUT

This loving God truly invades us, no longer as an idea or a thought, but as the Source of all life. He drives out of our hearts all vestige of sin and darkness and transforms us into His loving light. As we get caught up inside of God's invading energies of love, we find ourselves gradually being consumed by the Trinity's mutual love for each other and for us. We become a prism by which God can radiate His love to all that we touch. We become a magnifying glass, to use the example of the Gorlitz shoemaker and mystic, Jacob Boehme (+1624), that allows the rays of God's warm love to burst into flame and to enflame the world with godly love.

As we experience the transforming love of the triune God, we surrender more completely each day to be moulded by the interior action of the Trinity. Our filial abandonment to the operations of the Trinity is at once also a movement outwardly towards the world. From an anonymous world-community we move interiorly to meet the loving and personalize *We* community of Father, Son and Holy Spirit. The completion of that inner movement is an outward thrust back to the world community to be a servant throught whom

God can actualize a world community of *I, Thou* and *We*, that is the Body of Christ, the Church, ever conscious of being the Bride of Christ.

The degree of God's invasion of us, or rather of how much we surrender to allow His all-invading presence to transform us, is measured infallibly by the testimony of the fruit of the Holy Spirit produced in us as we relate toward other creatures (GA 5:22). Love, peace, joy, gentleness, kindliness, patience and forbearance are the result of our awareness that the Heavenly Father holds us in His two hands, Jesus Christ and His Spirit, and that He loves us, infinitely. We show the presence and influence of the indwelling Trinity by the simple faith we have in the goodness of others who also are "invaded" by God. We trust others because we have let go of the control over our own lives in our surrender to God's interior guidance.

Compassionate mercy moves us, as it did Jesus, to bind up the wounds and to embrace the homeless of this world. The love of God in us gives us a share in God's love which is "always patient and kind; it is never jealous; love is never boastful or conceited; it is never rude or selfish . . . it is always ready to excuse, to trust, to hope, and to endure whatever comes" (1 Co 13:4-7).

This cannot be done except by embracing the cross of self-denial and emptying ourselves, as Jesus did. It is to live fully our Baptism by dying to our self-containment to rise in the newness of the trinitarian life within us, to live a life of self-giving to others. It is to experience at every moment the power of God's Spirit who brings us human beings into a unity or communion of loving brothers and sisters of the only begotten Son of God who leads us to the Father of us all.

In a word, to be invaded by God is to allow God to invade the world by our being present to God who is everywhere present as loving, personalized energies. It is to become so emptied of our nothingness and sinfulness that the Trinity may pour out its richness of life upon the whole world. It is not only to find the Trinity living within us, but it is to make the world around us present to that same immanently present and loving Trinity.

The words of Teilhard de Chardin suggest a proper conclusion to this chapter:

> Seeing the mystic immobile, crucified or rapt in prayer, some may perhaps think that his activity is in abeyance or has left this earth: they are mistaken. Nothing in the world is more intensely alive and active than purity and prayer, which hang like an unmoving light between the universe and God. Through their serene transparency flow the waves of creative power, charged with natural virtue and with grace. What else but this is the Virgin Mary?[23]

banner - fruits of the HS.
page in PB
listing the fruits

*CHAPTER TWO*

# In Search of a Process

One of the greatest theologians of the Catholic Church is without a doubt St. Thomas Aquinas. His productivity in teaching and writing staggers our modern minds—and he died at the early age of 49! And yet, the scene of St. Thomas dying in the Cistercian Monastery of Fossa Nova in northern Italy on his way to the Council of Lyons is what I most like to remember about St. Thomas, the true theologian who had searched all his life to know God. Shortly before he died in that monastery, he knelt before the Crucified Lord. He reported to his secretary, Brother Reginald, that he had learned more theology on his knees in those fifteen minutes than from all the theology that he had ever studied and written about in his many tomes. There is a "logion" that says St. Thomas begged Reginald to throw into the fire everything that he had written about God. "All that," he said, "is valueless and as worthless as straw. It is nothing but mockery."

That "logion" is to me the most beautiful utterance of St. Thomas' whole life as a preacher, a master in theology, a spiritual man, a saint. Oh, the humor of God! It would have been an amazing thing on the lips of St. Francis of Assisi or of St. Bernard who had gone through such a mystical experience, but how much more amazing that it should have been said by St. Thomas Aquinas, the "Ox of Sicily," the eminent professor at Paris, the Doctor of the Church of his time and of all times, the pillar of Catholic scholastic theology!

But brother Thomas had a presentiment of something greater than what he was writing about in his many volumes. In his *Commentary on the Epistle to the Romans,* he had written: "There is, therefore, one thing concerning God which remains completely unknown in this life, namely, what God is."[1] He so often returned to that theme and did so in such an uncompromising manner that some of his commentators have been seriously annoyed by the obvious scantiness of knowledge of God that he concedes to man here below. "The mind remains in some kind of night of ignorance, of *unknowing,* but it is that very ignorance that unites us to Him most perfectly, since it is in the night that God dwells." St. Thomas did not arrive at this knowledge of the possibility of a higher knowledge by unknowing as he sat in class learning from St. Albert or as he wrote his great compendia of scholastic theology. He kept seeking and asking questions for many years before he could say and feel himself being united to Him, God, as if to a Stranger. That happened just before the veil was torn, before God would finally show Himself as He really is.

## A CRISIS IN THEOLOGY TODAY

On all levels of Christian life the faithful are searching for a more immediate experience of God. Western man is more and more turning toward Eastern religions in the hope of finding a different approach to reality. Descartes' "clear and distinct ideas" have given the West a rationalistic science of theology. Yet man hungers desperately for an immediate encounter with the God of Abraham, Isaac and Jacob.

The 70's have been marked by a unique interest in and experimenting with expansion of consciousness on the part of the ordinary person. No doubt the rise in anxieties and stresses in daily living, the inability to cope with the speed of urban life and the meaninglessness of it all has pushed most "seekers" into the area of transcendent, psychic experiences as a way to avoid mental illness and to survive from day to day.

Every religion has a built-in danger that allows the faithful to settle for the trappings, the extrinsic forms of worship and dogma instead of continuing to grow through an intensive searching in one's heart for the wild God of the desert who cannot be put into convenient boxes of concepts and doctrines. Western theology by and large has become reduced to a static form of objectifying God's transcendence by separating Him in His primary causality in all things from the created world in its createdness.

Dr. Louis Dupré characterizes this loss of true transcendence in theology in these words:

> From the sixteenth century on, however, reality became rapidly reduced to its objective, if not its physico-mathematical qualities. The one-sidedness of the new approach seriously impaired the mind's self-understanding and, for the same reason, its ability to conceive a genuine transcendence. It even reduced our view of nature. What Heidegger writes about Descartes goes also for his successors: the world turned into a presence-at-hand *(Vorhanden)*, that is, an exclusive object of manipulation, closed to contemplation.[2]

Thus in theological circles today there is a search for a new method, one that avoids the causal model of objective transcendence and combines in a paradoxical way God's immanence in the whole world with His awesome transcendence that cries out that He is so totally *der ganz Andere* that whatever we say about Him must somehow also be denied as not totally true as said.

All too often in the past, theologians advocated a "scientific" theology in which the method of theological study of Christianity was brought as closely as possible to that of the "positive" sciences. Such a scientific theology tended to be a ratio-critical study of its subject matter. Even when such a theology was predicated on a *theory-praxis* dialectic, there was a heavy selective appropriation of themes that avoided the dark sides of theology and Christian praxis in an apologetic attempt to win over other Christians to a distinctly "intramural" view of Christian theology.

Some theologians cry out for a more holistic approach between theory and praxis.[3] In such a dialectic between theory and praxis these two aspects of Christian life are in a historical process of interaction and in a process of constant change.

## A PROCESS THEOLOGY

To prepare for a presentation of the Greek Fathers' understanding of a theology of God's uncreated energies, I would like to present the modern thinking current among some Christian philosophers and theologians who embrace the process philosophy of Alfred North Whitehead. Through the strengths and weaknesses of such insights we can be in a better position to appreciate the theology of uncreated energies as presented in the theological writings of some of the Greek Fathers.

Process philosophy is a term which designates a broad movement in modern philosophy and, more particularly, a group of thinkers who focus in on an evolutionary world view and the temporal flow of experience. The name which has become most associated with this type of thought is Alfred North Whitehead, although one could include a whole variety of individuals ranging from Henri Bergson to Charles Hartshorne. I would like to focus, however, on Whitehead and those theologians who expound on his thought, particularly Daniel Day Williams, Norman Pittenger and Schubert Ogden.[4]

Process philosophy thinkers maintain that their discovery opens for Christian theology a way of conceiving God in historical-temporal terms. It seeks the "logos" of being:

> The biblical God acts in a history where men have freedom which they can misuse. He is at work in time, and it is just this which the theological tradition, conditioned by neo-platonic metaphysics has never been able to encompass.[5]

The first and perhaps basic assumption of Whitehead and process thinkers in general is that the world is a dynamic rather than a static reality. Human nature, for example, cannot be described as an immutable and unchanging thing. Man is a living, changing, developing creature. Likewise, the world of nature is not something static.

> Down to the lowest levels of matter, if we may so style them, this capacity for and presence of change and development is to be seen.[6]

Whitehead even describes an electron as a "society" or an "organism" marked by movement and activity. The world as a whole is both in process and is itself a process.

This leads to a second assumption which is basic to process thought. The world and all that is in it is an inter-related society of "occasions." There is no possibility of isolating one occasion from another so that each may be considered in itself alone. Into each given occasion there enter past events as well as present pressures and the "lure" of the future. A man, for example, cannot exist in complete isolation from other men, or from his own past history, or from any of the developments of mankind in general. In being "himself," he is all that has gone on within him and around him.

> We live in and we are confronted by a richly inter-connected, inter-related, inter-penetrative series of events, just as we ourselves are such a series of events.[7]

In process thought, as Whitehead develops it, there is given to us a variety of relationships which have played upon us and have brought about our experience in a particular way. The converging process brings this rather than that to a focus. What in older philosophy might have been seen as a chain of cause and effect is seen in a much richer understanding of occasions, pressures, movements and events which come to focus at this or that point.

For Whitehead, the thing which secures the identity of each particular occasion is its "subjective aim" which is proper to each series of occasions. There is an element of teleological concern in all process thought. This does not mean that this aim is conscious in each set of occasions (an acorn is certainly not aware of the "aim" which keeps it moving in its proper development), but what does keep things moving is the subjective aim which they possess. A consequence of these assumptions is the rejection of all those dualisms which would make simple divisions between mind and matter, natural and supernatural, etc.

Now let us look briefly at Whitehead's understanding of God. Whitehead has a close affinity to the classical metaphysical tradition. He wishes to maintain the eternal order in the mind of God, but he also wants to conceive reality, which includes God, as having a real history of concrete happenings.

Whitehead and those theologians who interpret his thinking have a great difficulty with what they understand to be traditional theology. Whitehead's most telling statement against the tradition is that "the Church gave God the attributes which belonged exclusively to Caesar."[8]

Theologians like Schubert Ogden argue that this traditional view of God is a central reason why modern man has turned away from God. The God of traditional, scholastic philosophy has no relevance for secular man. For process theologians:

> The whole character of traditional theism is defined by an essential one-sidedness or monopolarity. As it conceives God, he is so far from being the eminently relative One that he is denied to be really related to our life at all.[9]

In other words, God's relation with the world are purely external, of a transcendent objective nature, lacking totally any immanent relationship.

Process thinkers will admit that traditional theology does speak of God as having real relationships with His creation. God does freely create and judge all things and by His mercy bring everything to its final end. But this is seen as nothing more than a mere appearance.

In the final analysis, conceiving God as the Absolute of classical scholastic philosophy is an absolute repugnance to anyone who has a truly secular attitude toward life in this world. Since God is wholly absolute, nothing whatever can make the least difference to Him.

> God's perfection is in every sense statically complete, an absolute maximum, so we can no more increase Him by our best efforts than diminish him by our worst.[10]

According to Whitehead's main outline of his doctrine of God, there are two aspects of the divine nature. The first he calls the "primordial nature" of God. This is the ordered realm in which are found all the possibilities of values and meanings that are relevant to existence. Whitehead holds that this side of God's being does not change. It is present to Him in one perfect vision. For Whitehead, this aspect of God's nature has all the attributes which have been traditionally assigned to Him. Since it is eternal, it cannot be acted upon or suffer. The reason is that if there is a meaningful world in process, there must be something which sets the boundaries of how things can be related to one another.

For Whitehead, however, there is another aspect of God which he calls the "consequent nature." God's actuality involves concrete process. God shares with His creates a degree of freedom so that His inter-action with His creatures involves real inter-communication. What happens in the world is of concern to God. He responds concretely to every new event by taking it as a datum into a new phase of His own life and arranging it according to His vision. What remains fixed for God is the integrity of His aim which looks toward the fullness of life for the whole of creation.

It must be pointed out clearly that Whitehead does not identify God with the world process. Rather, He is the eternal structure which makes the world possible in the first place and which participates in each moment of the world's becoming. God is a conscious, personal being.

God is the one who gives an ordered pattern to the creative life of the world to bring new possibilities into existence. God holds the world together by offering His eternal structure to everything that happens and brings it into relation with the whole community of beins. God, however, does not destroy the freedom of creatures within this order. For Daniel Day Williams, process theology is a significant improvement on Augustine's thought:

> We avoid here one of the curious consequences of the Augustinian ontology which is that the world can add nothing to God. How can you add anything to absolute perfection? But in Whitehead's doctrine, every achievement of good, of value, of meaning in the world increases the richness of God's being.[11]

I have presented here, in a very summary form, a synopsis of modern process thought, following the philosophy of Whitehead. What I would like to do in the remaining part of this essay is to contrast this view with that of the doctrine of the "essence and energies of God" as seen by the Greek Fathers, climaxing with the synthesis of St. Gregory Palamas (1296-1369). I will try to show that there exists considerable similarity between process philosophy and the dynamic views of the Greek Fathers in regard to God's uncreated energies. The insights of such modern process thinkers are not completely unknown, therefore, in Christian theological circles and are not, therefore, so totally novel. If such process thinkers of our modern time had a greater familiarity with the Greek Fathers, they would not have had such difficulties with what they call "traditional theism." They seem to be unaware that there is a wealth that can be drawn from the Greek Fathers. A knowledge of this would enable them to bring together the transcendence and the immanence of the Christian God in a better way than they have done.

## NATURE AND THE SUPERNATURAL

Before we can see the nature of God's uncreated energies in interaction with us human beings, we must first see how the Greek Fathers conceived man's nature. In a word, I would like to sketch their theological anthropology as they theologized about man's nature from Holy Scripture.

In his history-making book, *Le surnaturel*, Henri de Lubac seeks to show that the early Fathers with their dynamic approach based on concrete, historical human nature, the only one that now exists, had never admitted a nature that was not at the same time by its very ontological makeup, as it came from the hand of God, dynamically in movement towards its supernatural end.[12] It would be wrong to assert that the Fathers denied the possibility of a pure nature, a human nature not having God as its final end. The Greek Fathers simply never thought of the problem, absorbed as they were with the historical order of the present economy of salvation. Not faced with the Pelagian heresy, as was St. Augustine, who bequeathed his important and subtle distinctions to Western theology to highlight the gratuity of God in being free and independent in His bestowal of grace on man, the Greek Fathers viewed the inter-relationship of nature and grace in terms of one continuous unfolding *process* of two different but not contradictory entities: man's ontological nature as God made him, with potencies that would be actuated with God's help only when the end was attained that God had destined for man, and God's gratuitous bestowal of the gift of Divine Life that drew out of the image according to which God created man a more perfect similitude to the perfect Image of God, the Divine Logos.[13]

What was the common understanding of the Fathers when they used the word *nature* ( φύσις )? The characterization of nature and grace as opposites in the *Imitation of Christ*[14] (where nature is depicted as being corrupt and tending always to vice, while grace is the elevating, infused force that allows the spiritual man to do good) would never have come from the pen of an Eastern Father. The starting point of such Fathers was different and found in Holy Scripture. Fundamentally, nature for the Fathers is the *opus Dei* as it comes from the hands of God. This work of God, with all of its hidden, unactuated possibilities, as Irenaeus, Origen, Gregory of Nyssa and the other Greek Fathers repeat constantly, is good. There is nothing in man's makeup that is evil.

But the nature of man partakes also of the end that the Creator had in mind in giving it existence. God did not create a nature in a vacuum but created for it an end towards which the nature tends through the free-will cooperating of man with the Creator. The whole man, body with all of its senses and passions, the soul with its intellect and will, all were created good by God. The whole scope of the spiritual life is to make a given, concrete human nature approximate that nature intended by God in His will-act of giving existence to it. Thus *nature* for the Greek Fathers is never a universal, abstract concept that can be applied equally to all human beings in a static, self-composed, independent existence, but it refers always to an ontological, existing being according to the given potencies and the plan of God with all His grace-full relationships given to a concrete person in order that he might fulfill God's salvific designs in his regard and thus attain his own perfect, *natural* self-realization.

Supernatural grace added to man in his regeneration into the new man by the reception in Baptism of Divine Life is not something superimposed, but, according to the Greek Fathers, it is the actuation of a potency that was there in the nature from creation. All good that can come to man must be "according to (κατά) nature." Vices or sins are the only things against nature, hence, unnatural, while the *supernatural* is eminently conformed to nature.

Christian perfection of a virtuous life in grace does not do violence to nature, but heals it, makes it grow, divinizes it without demanding any other sacrifice than a conversion, a *metanoia*, the uprooting of a will that goes against the creative will of God.

Only a free will act on the part of man is demanded by God in order that man receive the gifts of God that are contained in his nature as a seed contains all the perfections of the matured tree. St. Irenaeus of the second century has an apt expression: "Man is the receptacle of the goodness of God." If man consents by humbling himself to his true ontological place as a creature before his Creator, if he makes himself supple and malleable in the hands of the Divine Artist, God can make of him His *chef-d'oeuvre*, a true, loving child of God in union with the only Begotten Son, Jesus Christ, co-heir with Him of Heaven forever.[15]

This is all a work of God's love, freely given to man. God spills out His Love in activity in the creation of men and the universe, in the Incarnation of His Divine Son, Jesus Christ, in the Redemption by the God-Man of the whole human and subhuman cosmos, in the sanctification and final Parousia through the Holy Spirit. These are all actions of God prompted by the one constant act of love.

Love, in order to exist, in man or God, must always be loving, always pouring itself out from its own abundance, always giving of itself. It is thus through God's action of His loving us (and this we call grace in its most *primary* meaning according to the Greek Fathers) and in and through His life in us by our loving in return that we come to union with Love Himself. This is God in His loving, uncreated energies, as we will explain; it is the whole Trinitarian love in active, creative relationships with man. In this oneness of Love, we are united with every other human being created and loved by God. The nature of God is such that, while being one, it demands a plurality as objects of His love, of His giving. Love is the best word that St. John and any other human being could choose to describe God's relation to man. In man's constant response to this invitation of God's love consists all his greatness and fulfillment. It is our loving in return (always made possible through God's energizing grace) that divinizes us, brings us into a oneness in love so that God truly lives in us by participation.

"God is love and anyone who lives in love lives in God, and God lives in him" (1 Jn 4:16). Grace, therefore, is God loving His human creation and deifying it through His activity with human beings freely choosing the Way to the Truth that leads to Life that is Love Personified.

## IMAGE AND LIKENESS

The early Eastern Fathers built up not only a theology of divinization around the two terms found in Genesis 1:26 "according to our *image* and *likeness*": (εἰκών–ὁμοίωσις), but we find in their speculation about these two concepts the meeting of an integrated theology of Christ and the Trinity, creation and man, as well as a religious psychology of man, and a dynamic expression of the life of grace as a process in mutual love relationship between man and God. The Septuagint or Greek Old Testament does not say that man is the *image and likeness* of God. Man is made only *according* to the image, i.e., in Greek, St. Paul tells us that Jesus Christ is the Image of God:

> He is the image of the unseen God
> and the first-born of all creation,
> for in him were created
> all things in heaven and on earth:
> everything visible and everything invisible . . .
> all things were created through him and for
> him (Col 1:15-16).

Jesus Christ is God's Logos and in Him, God is gathering up His entire work, fulfilling it according to His original plan. Christ's work and the whole *real* progress in the universe, according to God's reckoning, are measured in terms of the restoration of the first creation through Christ's activities in the cosmos. Irenaeus puts the end of man and the universe simply in the following words:

> For this is why the Word of God is man, and this is why the Son of God became the Son of Man, that man might possess the Word, receive adoption, and become the son

of God. In no other way could we receive incorruptibility and immortality except by being united with incorruptibility and immortality. But how could we be united with incorruptibility and immortality unless incorruptibility and immortality had first become what we are, in order that what is corruptible might be absorbed in incorruptibility and what is mortal by immortality, that so we might receive the adoption of sons?[16]

*CHAPTER THREE*

# Knowing the Unknowable God

Karl Barth had a great love for Mozart and his music. Each day for years, he played some Mozart music before going to work on his dogmatic works because Barth hoped that such transcendent music would unconsciously awaken in him the hidden, sophianic music that comes in tune with the divine and cosmic music that saves speculative theology by an experience of the ineffable in love.[1] In his awareness of the *apophatic* element, the inexpressible that can, however, be apprehended in a religious experience, Barth was in touch with the spirit of the early Eastern Fathers in their best theologizing works.

The early Fathers of the Church feared the formulation of dogmas, since that tended to reduce the living faith of the Gospels to "a system of thought." St. Hilary of Poitiers, a Father of the Latin Church, wrote in the fourth century that which was held universally among the Greek Fathers.

> The guilt of the heretics and blasphemers compels us to undertake what is unlawful, to scale arduous heights, to

> speak of the ineffable, and to trespass upon forbidden places. And since by faith alone we should fulfill what is commanded, namely, to adore the Father, to venerate the Son with Him, and to abound in the Holy Spirit, we are forced to raise our lowly words to subjects which cannot be described. By the guilt of another we are forced into guilt, so that what should have been restricted to the pious contemplation of our minds is now exposed to the dangers of human speech.[2]

The Eastern Fathers unanimously agree on the importance of a *cataphatic* or positive, deductive, affirming approach to theology. They see such an approach as yielding a certain positive knowledge about God and man and the world, but such an approach is an imperfect way and must be complemented by the *apophatic* approach. The positive approach to theology is a descent from the superior degrees of being to the inferior. It is to speak of God through His causality upon the material effects of His created order, including man and the entire material world. About God in His activities toward creation the theologian can speak and ascribe to Him certain attributes. These are the *epinoiai* of Origen. Pseudo-Dionysius describes some of the areas that cataphatic theology deals with and points out that the details and images and words tend to become more copious and diffused than in the apophatic approach. Let me quote from him his general description of the work of cataphatic theology:

> In the treatise on *Divine Names*, we have considered the meaning, as concerning God, of the titles of Good, of Being, of Life, of Wisdom, of Power, and of such other names as are applied to Him; further, in *Symbolical Theology*, we have considered what are the metaphorical titles drawn from the world of sense and applied to the nature of God; what is meant by the material and intellectual images we form of Him, or the functions and instruments of activity attributed to Him; what are the places where He dwells and the raiment in which He is adorned; what is meant by God's anger, grief, and

indignation, or the divine inebriation; what is meant by God's oaths and threats, by His slumber and waking; and all sacred and symbolic representations. And it will be observed how far more copious and diffused are the last terms than the first, for the theological doctrine and exposition of the *Divine Names* are more brief than the *Symbolical Theology*.[3]

## THE NEGATIVE WAY

In the history of theology certain theologians have yielded to the temptation of theologizing exclusively in terms of positive theology. Such an example were Eunomius and his followers, the Eunomians, who pushed the cataphatic theology and the ability of man to form rational concepts to the limit of heresy. They held that the essence of God could be clearly known by man. The divine essence could be apprehended intellectually and exhaustively in the mere fact that one accepted the supposed revelation of God as "not engendered." Once one "saw" the truth of this postulate that the Father alone, the "not engendered," was God, one entered into the full light of the divine essence and God Himself had no more light than this.

In such a system the Son and the Holy Spirit are both creatures of God and Christianity is emptied of all mystery. Man by his intellect can attain and apprehend all there is to know of God. By destroying the immanence of the mysterious indwelling Trinity, Eunomius destroyed also the transcendence of the one God in His unknowable essence.

Against such thinking the great Cappadocian theologians, St. Basil, St. Gregory of Nazianzus and St. Gregory of Nyssa, developed an apophatic theology as a necessary corrective. This is not merely the *via negationis* of St. Thomas Aquinas who, with the Cappadocians and all other true Christian theologians down through the centuries, insists on a negative theology to correct the affirmative theology in the manner of attributing perfections to God. Such a method is necessary to correct the *modus significandi*, the manner of speaking in human concepts which never can exhaust the infinite perfections found in God. Such a theology attempts to speak of God by what He is *not* rather than by what He is.

For the Cappadocians, God is superior to all other essences. The biblical description of God, the *One who is* (ὁ ὤν) expresses the divinity that is infinite and above all intelligibility on the part of finite creatures. God is the only truly authentic being which is opposed to all other non-being. Such an *antinomic* approach would logically lead us to a rigorous nominalism or agnosticism as in the case of Barlaam of Calabria in his 14th century controversy with St. Gregory Palamas. Antinomic apophatic theology asserts that the negativity with which one approaches God cannot be surpassed. The last word is a "not."[4]

But the "father" of Christian mysticism, St. Gregory of Nyssa, opens theology up to the positive elements of the apophatic approach. He develops in his writings a mystical theology that would form the basis of that dialectical, mystical experience of God, a knowing but not knowing, that Pseudo-Dionysius evolved and bequeathed to Maximus the Confessor, to Scotus Erigena, to the 14th century Rhenish and Flemish mystics such as Meister Eckhart, Tauler, Suso and Jan Ruysbroeck and to the anonymous writer of the 14th century English classic, *The Cloud of Unknowing*.

Such a dialectical, mystical apophatic theology holds that the "not" is the beginning of a knowledge of God by experience. It is based on the impossibility of defining God by human concepts but not on the impossibility of somehow knowing Him. Such an approach is based not on an absolute *no*, but on a relative *no*, a "pas encore," to quote Cyprian Kern.[5] There is a question of true theological knowledge, but it is more in the experience of God as giving Himself to the repentant mystic who approaches God in a sate of brokenness and interior poverty of spirit. Vladimir Lossky describes the the knowledge of God beyond all conceptualization that St. Gregory of Nyssa called *theognosis*, knowledge taught by God.

> . . . having failed to recognize the One it desires among the intelligible and incorporeal beings, and abandoning all that it finds, it recognizes the One it is seeking as the only One he does not comprehend . . . Union with God is presented as a path which goes beyond vision, intelligence to the area where knowledge is suppressed and love alone remains—or rather where *gnosis* becomes *agape.*[6]

We must note that the overwhelming infinity of God is nevertheless an experienced presence of God to the contemplative. But the modality of recognizing this presence is a new and higher form of knowledge that surpasses the powers and experiences of man. Thus St. Gregory resorts to such paradoxical terms as "luminous darkness," "sober inebriation," etc. He describes this presence without seeing in his *Commentary on the Song of Songs:*

> The Bride is surrounded with the divine night in which the Bridegroom comes near without showing Himself. . . but by giving the soul a certain sense of His presence while fleeing from clear knowledge.[7]

This is the positive, dialectical side to the apophatic theology of the Eastern Fathers. The Incomprehensible One is present and is experienced by the Christian. It is this very presence that is spoken of. It is that very transcendence that brings darkness to man's own reasoning powers. The emphasis is not on the incapacity of man, but rather on the overwhelming infinity of God that is nevertheless present.

Presence and transcendence are one in apophatic theology. In paradoxical fashion, the closer one gets to union with God, the more blinding God becomes. This is not a matter of the knowledge of God becoming more abstruse but of the nature of God itself becoming more present. That presence brings to man the realization of the absolute awesomeness of the goal of his earthly journey.

## THE SPIRITUAL SENSES

The theology of the spiritual senses is one of St. Gregory's ways of expressing that "going-beyond-oneself" into new knowledge given by God to the purified Christian. The spiritual senses which are the result of purification, are in man as the physical senses, which are bounded by purification. The spiritual senses are the activities that are analogous to the physical but are, nevertheless, spiritual. They are the operations of the spiritual man, the interior man, the true *theologos*, the theologian. They are the operations of the image of God in man. Gregory describes this as a going beyond oneself, as in ecstasy, drunkenness, sleep and even passion. Perhaps the meaning of the spiritual senses can best be described by the examples he himself uses.

He speaks of Abraham in ecstasy before the "God who transcends all knowable symbols."[8] Having purified himself and studied all that there was to know of the divine attributes (the cataphatic approach) Abraham finds faith in the Transcendent God. It is this that is ecstasy:

> And so, after this ecstasy, which comes upon him as a result of these lofty visions, Abraham returned once more to his human frailty; *I am*, he admits, dust and ashes, mute, inert, incapable of explaining rationally the Godhead that my mind has seen.[9]

After purification and study, God comes to Abraham in faith and this carries Abraham beyond himself in that he sees himself as nothing and inert. This ecstasy is really brought on from outside. Passivity is this strange activity. Purification and illumination do not bring on ecstasy but rather faith that God comes to man. The coming of the vision is what makes Abraham realize that he is nothing before God. The incomprehensibility of God overawes and mutes the fleshly mind and senses.

In ecstasy David also "cried out in those famous words: "Every man is a liar."[10] David has become drunk in his spiritual senses and sees the illusion that is in man's senses. In that same passage, Gregory notes that Paul and Peter also become inebriated and when ecstasy came to them they were carried out of themselves. By ecstasy man is carried beyond his normal state into the spiritual, but really this state is man's rightful place.

Ecstasy, therefore, does not mean in apophatic theology what it means to us in the language of popular mysticism. It is best expressed by "going out of oneself" because of the overpowering presence of the Infinite. It is entering into new knowledge through the "luminous darkness," an excess of light that is too much for the mind. It is also described as a "watchful sleep" or the loss of all the senses and every bodily motion.

The expression "vertigo" is used in the *Commentary on the Canticle of Canticles* and conveys for St. Gregory of Nyssa the same basic meanings as the other expressions. The closeness of the transcendent is not speculative but expresses a real anguish, like that of one on a high cliff, who steps near the edge and finds himself with no footing. Applying the image to the realization of God's presence, St. Gregory says:

> And thus the soul, slipping at every point from what cannot be grasped, becomes dizzy and perplexed and returns once again to what is connatural to it, content now to know merely this about the Transcendent, that it is completely different from the nature of things that the soul knows.[11]

## THE ASCENT TO MOUNT SINAI

It is especially in St. Gregory's treatise on the *Life of Moses* that we have a full presentation of the soul's journey up the mountain to meet God in the darkness of unknowing. In this work, Gregory develops the meaning of darkness. Although it does mean, as I have already said, that man possesses an incapacity to know God intimately, it primarily means that God is absolutely unfathomable, the fullness of being, and man can "understand" this only in the darkening of man's controlled faculties of intellection.

Like Moses' ascent of Mount Sinai, the movement of the individual towards enlightenment begins in darkness of sin. He sees a ray of the light of God that beckons him to leave the foothills and start climbing upward. The higher stages are degrees of his entrance into the darkness of God's incomprehensibility. Gregory states this in his *Commentary on the Canticle of Canticles:*

> Our initial withdrawal from wrong and erroneous ideas of God is a transition from darkness to light. Next comes a closer awareness of hidden things, and by this the soul is guided through sense phenomena to the world of the invisible. And this awareness is a kind of cloud, which overshadows all appearances, and slowly guides and accustoms the soul to look toward what is hidden. Next the soul makes progress through all these stages and goes on higher, and as she leaves behind all that human nature can attain, she enters within the secret chamber of the divine knowledge, and here she is cut off on all sides by the divine darkness. Now she leaves outside all that can be grasped by sense or by reason, and the only thing left for her contemplation is the invisible and the incomprehensible.[12]

It should be noted that for St. Gregory of Nyssa the movement is not from darkness to light solely, but it is a continued process from darkness to light and then to darkness and again to light.[13]

## EPECTASIS: LOVE ALWAYS GROWING

A key doctrine of St. Gregory of Nyssa that keeps his apophatic dialectical movement from darkness to light, from absence to presence of God, from absolute transcendence of God to His immanence, present to man in loving union, is his teaching on what he calls *epectasis.* This means a "stretching out," an exceeding of one's level of attained love of God, based on St. Paul's statement: "I strain ahead for what is still to come (Phil 3:13). The love of God is a force in man expanding his being and making him infinitely capable of possessing God in an unending process of greater and greater growth, both in his life through contemplation and also in the life to come. Gregory describes true perfection as "never to stop growing towards what is better and never to place any limit on perfection."[14]

The reasons he gives for this continued growth are first, that Beauty, God Himself, is infinite. The second reason is that the Beautiful is of such a nature that the desire for it can never be fully satisfied.[15] Gregory writes:

> The soul that looks up towards God and conceives that good desire for His eternal beauty, constantly experiences an ever new yearning for that which lies ahead and her desire is never given its full satisfaction.[16]

This stretching forth to possess more and more the Unpossessable is described in antinomical terms. For Gregory, the unrest, the stretching forth to higher perfection and greater assimilation into the Absolute, such motion toward greater being is the same as stability.[17] Motion for Gregory means more than moving from one stage to another of perfection. The very transcendence of God is the reason that perfection itself is constant motion. God is eternally at rest; yet He exists always in an outgoing motion of love to share Himself with the other. Thus after the contemplative soul has been purified of all taint of self-absorption, God attracts it continually to

> keep rising ever higher and higher, stretching with its desire for heavenly things to those that are before (Phil 3:13), as St. Paul tells us, and thus it will always continue to soar ever higher. . . and thus the soul moves ceaselessly upwards, always reviving its tension for its onward flight by means of the progress it has already realized. Indeed, it is only spiritual activity that nourishes its force by exercise; it does not slacken its tension by action but rather increases it.[18]

## A MYSTICAL THEOLOGY

It was, however, to the mysterious personage that history has called Dionysius the Areopagite that these insights of St. Gregory of Nyssa would be handed down in the famous, small treatise called *The Mystical Theology.*[19] In this treatise, apophatic theology reaches its peak in transforming theology into a contemplation of the mysteries of revelation. Mystical theology is not a branch of theology dealing with the aspects of higher contemplation and hence applicable only to a few gifted persons. By placing the accent so completely on the unknowability of God's essence without yielding to agnosticism or a refusal to allow a real knowledge of God by a higher knowledge attainable by man as a gift from God, the Greek Fathers, whose doctrine Pseudo-Dionysius aptly summarizes, saw theology never as abstract and

> working through concepts, but contemplative: raising the mind to those realities which pass all understanding. . . It is not a question of suppressing the antinomy by adapting dogma to our understanding, but of a change of heart and mind enabling us to attain to the contemplation of the reality which reveals itself to us as it raises us to God, and unites us, according to our several capacities, to Him.[20]

In a classical passage, Pseudo-Dionysius describes the mystical side of true apophatic theology:

> Nevertheless, he (Moses) did not attain to the Presence of God Himself; he saw not Him (for He cannot be looked upon), but the Place where He dwells. And this I take to signify that the divinest and highest things seen by the eyes or contemplated by the mind are but the symbolical expressions of those that are immediately beneath Him who is above all. Through these, His incomprehensible Presence is manifest upon those heights of His Holy Places; that then it breaks forth, even from that which is seen and that which sees, and plunges the mystic into the Darkness of Unknowing, whence all perfection of understanding is excluded, and he is enwrapped in that which is altogether intangible and noumenal, being wholly absorbed in Him who is beyond all, and in none else (whether himself or another); and through the inactivity of all his reasoning powers is united by his highest faculty to Him who is wholly unknowable; thus by knowing nothing he knows that which is beyond his knowledge.[21]

## A LIVING THEOLOGY

Through a correct apophatic theology there is no opposition to cataphatic theology. It encourages a positive theology expressed through rational concepts, but it constantly tells positive theologians that the expressions used by them are not really the way such and such a perfection or relation exists in God. It stimulates them to open up to the mystery of a living contact with the immanent God who comes in a living experience.

The apparent conflicts between a speculative theology and that of a more mystical, experiential nature are resolved or made "livable" in the Liturgy of the Church, the experiential drama of dogma that takes the faithful into the heart of mystery to meet the living God of Abraham, Isaac and Jacob beyond any concepts.

The conflicts between a reasoned theology and an apophatic mystical approach are resolved in the living liturgical prayer. "No language knows how to praise You worthily and the mind, vaster than the world, becomes dizzy in celebrating You."[22] Dogmatic, speculative theology can tell us distinctions between substance and accidents and work out for us a theory of transubstantiation, but it is only in the immediate experience of celebrating the Eucharist and in receiving the Bread of Life that we come into a resolution of the antinomies of how eternity and time can meet, how Divinity can be joined with humanity, how Jesus Christ is both true God and true man eternally in glory and yet always coming into our lives to touch our human bodies with His glorious Body and Blood, how we are Church, many members and yet each member uniquely loved by God, waiting for the full eschaton to come and yet in the Eucharist it has begun.

For one who has experienced the living theology so present in the Byzantine Holy Week and Easter Services, the reconciliation of cataphatic and apophatic theology is an experience that brings together antinomies and allows us human beings to live in the power of such antinomies which function at the heart of our most transcendent, human experiences. On the vigil of Easter, when the church is flooded with lighted candles and the priest sings out: "Christ is risen! He is truly risen!'" one experiences the new victory of Christ over death. He finds it easier to believe also that the same "divinizing process" has already begun in his life and in those praying with him.

Not only do we believe it to be possible, as when we recite the Nicene-Constantinopolitan Creed each Sunday, but we know it through experience, through a liturgical and ecclesiastical situation. "The God-Man lies in sabbath repose and yet is risen. Creatures lament, the sun hides its rays, stars are lightless, but for us, this Sabbath is blessed among all since Christ sleeps, to arise on the third day."

## BARLAAM AND GREGORY PALAMAS

St. Gregory Palamas, a monk on Mount Athos in the 14th century, met up with the writings of Barlaam, an Orthodox monk born in Calabria, Italy and educated in the scholastic method of the West. A clash between the spirit of the Renaissance and the traditional monastic spirituality took place that would do much to consolidate the two positions of Eastern versus Western theology and prevent any serious theological dialogue since that time for the past six centuries. We will see later on how these two clashed on the problem of God's relationships with us through His uncreated energies. But their initial dispute centered on our knowledge of God. Can God be perceived by man? Is there any sure and immediate knowledge other than that derived from sense knowledge?

Palamas, in line with his predecessors, the Greek Fathers, especially the Cappadocian Fathers, held firmly to the positive, affirming theology. But he insists on a more perfect knowledge, one that is not derived analogically from creatures but a knowledge about God given to us by God. This knowledge is rooted in the Incarnation, for if the Word of God had not been incarnate, we would not have known God in a direct and intimate way, but only as contemplated mediately through creatures. He writes:

> We have all known the Son through the voice of the Father who announced this doctrine from on high, and the Holy Spirit, the inexpressible light itself, has assuredly shown us that here is the well-Beloved of the Father. The Son Himself has manifested the name of His Father and has promised that after His return to Heaven, He would send us the Holy Spirit who has descended, remained with us and declared and taught us the whole truth.[23]

This knowledge for Palamas, who best summarizes for us the consistent teaching of the Greek Fathers on the apophatic, mystical theology, is a unique reality. "Whatever name we give it—union, vision, sensation, knowledge, intellection, illumination—it cannot properly be applied to it, or rather, cannot adequately be applied to it."[24]

To describe it, Palamas also uses concepts which the Bible and the Fathers before him had made familiar: the "vision of the heart," the "divine eye," and the "holy sensation." For Palamas, these are different ways of expressing a single reality, that of the supernatural faculty possessed by all Christians to know God.

Barlaam found himself opposed to cataphatic theology and in favor of some form of apophatic dialectical theology. He taught that God was indeed unknowable, but that His incomprehensibility was a question of the limits of man's reason and not primarily a question of the nature of God. The knowledge of which he speaks, therefore, seems to be a form of conceptual knowledge, but because God's essence is too great for man's mind, it remains unknown. He is a nominalist in the tradition of William of Occam and holds that since all knowledge, i.e., conceptual knowledge, begins with the senses and since God surpasses sense knowledge He is unknowable. Thus Barlaam was to contend that the best form of knowledge that man possesses is philosophy or "the knowledge of beings" and their concepts. Theology which held out the hope of knowing God was a futile enterprise and an apophatic theology that taught an experiential knowledge on the part of man toward God was truly, for him, a heresy.

It is interesting that both Barlaam and Palamas read Pseudo-Dionysius and yet came up with diametrically opposed views. Barlaam thought that he had found in Dionysius' writings the confirmation of his agnosticism.[25] While he read Dionysius with a nominalist point of view, Palamas read him in the broader context of the entire Christian tradition and found in him a confirmation of the possibility of knowledge of and union with God. Palamas brought his "Christological corrective" (to quote Meyendorff's phrase) to bear on the writings of Dionysius and thus he kept open the door to union with God in Christ. For Palamas, two areas had to be defended to be true to the Christian theological tradition: on the one hand, the doctrine that man can indeed participate in God, and on the other, that God is beyond knowledge.

These positions would seem to involve him in contradiction at one point or another, but the case is not such, for what Palamas meant by "knowledge" is not what Barlaam meant. It refers not to conceptual knowledge but to a union of life and of love at the core of one's existence. For Palamas, the vision of God is a positive thing, but not positive after the fashion of cataphatic theology where the content of what one sees supposedly can be expressed in concepts. It is a negative thing in one sense, but not merely negative in the sense of negating the limitations of reason. Mystical vision is negative by asserting that *because of the nature of God* and not primarily because of the human intellect, God cannot be known in any concept. The positive aspect of the vision of God is likewise not the positivity of a concept but of God's free and loving revelation of Himself in faith.

St. Gregory Palamas summarizes his teaching on man's knowledge of God that, as we have shown, is in continuity with the best theologizing on this subject by the early Greek Fathers:

> For those who have been purified by *hesychia* know that the Divine surpasses these contemplations and these initiations and so possesses that grace supra-intelligible and super-additional in a way that surpasses us; they possess it not because they do not see after the fashion of those who practise negative theology, but because there is in the very vision which they know, something which surpasses vision, by undergoing negation and not be conceiving it. Just as the act of undergoing and seeing divine things differs from cataphatic theology and is superior to it, so does the act of undergoing negation in spiritual visions, negation linked to the transcendence of the Object, differ from negative theology and is superior to it.[26]

There are several points that need to be stressed through the content of this passage that have great impact on our theology for today.

1. Negative theology does not of itself suffice, for it is merely a negative of the knowledge of beings and is not yet a knowledge of God.

2. The knowledge which the Christian has of God is religious and existential, not conceptual.

> It is not to any formal criterion, defined by Aristotle, that one owes the knowledge that God is unknowable, but through a religious experience, which may be in part due to a true understanding of beings, but which equally constitutes a revelation of the living God.[27]

The existential ways in which one may "know" God are the keeping of His commandments and above all prayer. "Prayer offers (this union). . .being the link between the rational creature and God."[28]

3. Such knowledge, therefore, is not based on a split between the senses and the intellect, as in a Platonic view, but rather between the created and the uncreated. Palamas

must be viewed as a holistic theologian who saw the imageness of God not only in man's intellect but in the whole person, made up of body, soul and spirit relationships. He writes: "The word Man. . . is not applied to either soul or body separately, but to both together, since together they have been created in the image of God."[29]

4. The knowledge of God which the Christian possesses in Christ is a direct face-to-face vision, and not, as Barlaam and his followers held, a vision mediated by angels. Palamas, contrary to a teaching that seemingly was credited to Pseudo-Dionysius, namely, that angels mediated man's knowledge of God, taught that the coming of Christ had inverted the natural order of the universe (in which angels served as mediators between men and God) and had substituted in its place a totally new hierarchy wherein men surpassed the angels and had a direct vision of God in Christ.

5. This knowledge, finally, is no mere "symbolic" knowledge, but a real knowledge of God as He is in Himself. Against the "intellectual symbolism" which Barlaam held to explain the mediated knowledge that man had of God, Palamas held that God was present in Christ. He Himself had broken down the separation between the "up there" and the "down here," and Christ had made it possible for God to be forever present in man's material world. In Palamas' incarnational view of history, Christ Himself was the symbol uniting man and God. It was Christ and His Holy Spirit that illumined the hesychast mystic. Jesus Christ, for Palamas, is the "sacrament" of God making God present to us in a knowing experience directly of God.

Let us now turn to the divine energies whereby the Holy Trinity, Father, Son and Spirit, touch us human beings and communicate themselves to us in a real, direct way that still preserves the unknowability of God in His essence. It is in his articulation of this dialectical antinomy that we can gain great insight for our modern theology that yearns for knowledge beyond concepts. We have seen how Palamas and the other preceding Greek Fathers maintained that God is in Himself, in His *essence*, unknowable and "non-participable" while at the same time God in His *manifestations* or *energies* is knowable.

> The Divine substance is incommunicable and yet is, in a certain sense, communicated; we partake of the nature of God and yet at the same time we do not partake of it at all. So we must maintain both (affirmations) and lay them down as the standard of piety.[30]

*CHAPTER FOUR*

# The Uncreated Energies

We have thus far seen that Eastern Christian theology has developed the distinction between the Divine Essence and God's uncreated energies as a means of explaining how God's being is unknowable by man and yet God does communicate Himself to man in a new knowing and a new participation through His energies. The energies are God's mode of existing in relationship to His created world, especially to man. Such a distinction is not often made use of in Western Christianity where God also is believed to be absolute and essentially unknowable. Nevertheless, He does relate Himself to the created order and so is knowable.

The importance of this distinction is seen in the Christian teaching of grace and the doctrine of deification or the sanctification of man. We have already pointed out the dangers of an Augustinian or Platonistic dichotomy between the two areas of nature and supernature.[1] In a concluding chapter, we will point out the consequences in theology, especially in the area of grace, of the doctrine of the uncreated energies. The aim of this chapter is to present, as clearly as possible, the unanimous teaching of the early Greek Fathers, climaxed by the synthesis made by St. Gregory Palamas, on the uncreated energies of God.[2]

Eastern Christian theologians from earliest time appealed to Holy Scripture to substantiate their claims for the distinction between God's essence and His energies. They appeal to Habakkuk to describe God's glory, brightness, light, rays and power that are manifested to men.

> Eloah is coming from Teman,
> and the Holy One from Mount Paran.
> His majesty veils the heavens,
> the earth is filled with his glory.
> His brightness is like the day,
> rays flash from his hands,
> that is where his power lies hidden
>
> (Hab 3:3-4).

Other references in Scripture are quoted, e.g.: Ps 36:9; Jr 23:24; Gn 17:22-23; 1 Tm 6:16 and 2 P 1:4. The Logos is spoken of by the early Fathers as the divine idea and energy, showing itself in creation. As has been pointed out, the Cappadocian Fathers, Basil, Gregory of Nazianzus and Gregory of Nyssa, in the polemical writings against the Eunomians write a great deal in an attempt to maintain the absolute transcendence of the unknowable essence of God and the relationships of God to His creatures. In their writings, the origin of their doctrine on the energies of God is evidently trinitarian. In defence of the mystery of the Trinity and in their elucidation of it, these Cappadocians insisted on the distinction between the divine essence and the energies. Jesus Christ, against Eunomius, who denied His divinity, and the Holy Spirit truly were a part of the divine essence and all three, having a common nature, produce identical divine energies *ad extra*, outside of the Trinitarian nature of the one Godhead.

St. Basil shows how the unapproachable and unknowable

essence of God can be, however, experienced through the energies of the divine nature:

> If it were possible to contemplate the divine nature itself in itself and find out what is proper to it and what is foreign through what appears, we would be in no need at all of words or other signs for the comprehension of what is sought. But because it is higher than the understanding of the things sought, and we reason parting from certain signs about things that evade our memory, it is of all necessity that we be conducted by the *energies* to the research of the divine nature.[3]

Basil also says: "For His (God's) energies descend down to us while His essence remains inaccessible."[4]

St. Gregory of Nazianzus, the Theologian, influenced greatly the thinking of Gregory Palamas. He wrote less in the context of polemics than the other two Cappadocians did and gives us a clearer doctrine of the energies. In defending the divinity of the Holy Spirit he describes the energies as an accident and not part of God's very own essence, and therefore he concludes that the Holy Spirit cannot be the energy of God coming down to us since the Spirit cannot be an accident.[5]

In using the image of Moses going up to Mount Sinai and being clothed in the cloud, Gregory writes:

> I was running, as if to seize God, and thus I ascended to the mountain, and penetrated the cloud having got inside far from matter and material things, gathered up into myself as much as possible. And when I looked, with difficulty, I saw the backside of God, and this while concealed in the stone, in the Word Incarnate for our cause; and looking a little further on, not upon the first and pure nature, known to itself, I mean to the Trinity and that which lies inside the first veil, and is concealed by the Cherubim, but the last one, which reaches us.[6]

Here is the basis for what we will point out in the writings of Palamas as his distinction between a "higher" (ὑπερκειμένη) and a "lower" (ὑφειμένη) Divinity, between the essence of the Godhead and the energies of the whole Godhead. This second, lower Divinity is multiple in its energetic relationships to the created world while the former is simple and one. The essence is incommunicable, while the energies are communicable and divisable. The favorite image of the sun emitting its rays to the earth is used by St. Gregory of Nyssa and will be repeated by all the succeeding Eastern theologians, especially by Palamas.

> Because the humility of our nature accepts not to be elevated above its proper measures, and to touch the supereminent nature of the all-high, for this reason dropping to our weakness his man-loving power, as far as it is possible for us to receive, thus distributes his grace and beneficiency. As the sun, according to the divine dispensation, temperating the vigor and sincerity of its rays by the intermediate air, emits to those receiving it a proportionate splendor and heat, remaining by itself unapproachable to the weakness of our nature, thus also the divine power, by a similarity to the given example, infinitely surpassing our nature and inaccessible to participation . . . gives to the human nature what is in her power to receive.[7]

## THE FORTHGOING OF GOD

What Palamas would call simply "energy," Pseudo-Dionysius would call by various attributes showing how God goes forth toward His created world to share His being or unlimited perfections. Dionysius was not considering in disputation as Palamas did against Barlaam the energies of God as really distinct from the simplicity of God's essence, but the same doctrine is found in his rather general descriptions of God's loving self-giving to mankind. Some of the Areopagite's expressions indicating God's energies are the following: God's *forthgoing* ( πρόοδος ) or manifestation of light, moved by the Father,[8] the *manifestation of God*, given harmoniously,[9] the divine *illumination*, or the *ray* of God ( ἀκτῖνα ) as the "super-substantial ray"[10] and finally, the *distribution* (μετάδοσις).

With such language Pseudo-Dionysius preserves the distinction between God's simplicity in essence and His "manifestations" in sharing His being in love with mankind. This is clearly seen in his phrase: "Providence and goodness participated by the beings, forthgoing from God who is outside all participation and overflowing with liberal profusion."[11]

The aim of man is union with God. From the part of God, Dionysius always speaks of the unifying power of His manifestations. A summary of his teaching on energies is found in his *Celestial Hierarchy:*

> All forthgoing of manifestation of light moved by the Father, attaining us through pure goodness, fills us anew as an up-elevating, unifying power, and converts us to the assembling unity of the Father, and His deifying simplicity.[12]

The end of our human lives is to attain "mystical knowledge," the summit of God's sharing Himself with us. Here we see Dionysius' understanding that God's energetic action towards us is completely gratuitous on His part. It is not man who raises himself to such a state but God's freely-given energies which work in man. Man must offer no obstacle to this action. In one of the most famous passages in the Dionysian corpus, we see how holy minds come to enjoy a union devoid of confusion, yet enter into a true participation with God's action as illuminator:

> . . . leave behind the sense and the operations of the intellect, and all things sensible and intellectual, and all

> things in the world of being and non-being, that thou mayest arise, by unknowing, towards the union, as far as is attainable, with Him who transcends all being and all knowledge. For by the unceasing and absolute renunciation of thyself and of all things, thou mayest be borne on high, through pure and entire self-abnegation, into the superessential Radiance of the Divine Darkness.[13]

This union by participation is a mystery. How can God share His being with man in such a way that man really participates in God's divinity without at the same time becoming God? This is the mystery of *theosis*, the divinization process of grace whereby the Christian is brought into a loving union with God through the divine energies, and still God retains His complete superessential being. Part of this mystery of how individuals really do experience the full divinity and yet each individual experiences God in His energies according to different proportions is stated in Dionysius' expression: "It is all the divinity completely which is participated by each participator, and by none in any part."[14]

To maintain such an antinomy Dionysius gives us a principle repeated often by Palamas whenever he seeks to reconcile apparent contradictions, at least that which seems to be such to the human mind. He writes: "Divine things should be understood in a God-fitting manner."[15] It is this which theologians must ever keep in mind that alone will resolve all apparent contradictions and justify all antinomies in divine things. No distinction humanly made can adequately describe the distinction between God's simplicity and essence and His participable self-giving in His energies. Let us look more closely at the system that St. Gregory Palamas developed from the writings of such Greek Fathers as mentioned above, especially from the writings of St. Gregory of Nazianzus and Pseudo-Dionysius.

## PARTICIPATION IN GOD'S LIFE

We have already pointed out how Gregory Palamas insisted with all of his predecessors on the unknowability of God. Yet he strongly asserts that man does indeed know and participate in God through Christ. "But there is one fact which stands distinct with reference to this transcendence: the complete and unadulterated existence in us of Jesus."[16] We are at the crucial node of Palamas' thought when we approach the question of the knowability and participability of God in and through His energies. The intensity of his concern for this problem of the possibility of the Christian's having a share in God's nature by participation in His energies is shown by the vigorous manner in which he tackles the question:

> Since man can participate in God and since the super-essential essence of God is absolutely unparticipable, there is a certain something between the unparticipable essence and the participants, which permits them to participate in God. And if you suppress that which is between the unparticipable God and the participants . . . oh, what a void!—you separate us from God by destroying the bond and establishing a great uncrossable abyss between God on the one hand and creation and the governing of creatures on the other. We must then seek another God who possesses not only His own proper end within Himself, His own proper energy and His own proper Godhead, but one who is a good God—for thus it will no longer suffice for Him to exist only for the contemplation of Himself—, not only perfect, but surpassing all fullness; thus, in effect, when, in His goodness, He will wish to do good, He will be able to do it; He will be not only immobile, but He will put Himself into motion; He will thus be present for all with His manifestations and His creative and providential energies; in one word, we must seek a God in whom we

> can have a share in one way or another, so that by participating in Him, each one of us may receive, in the manner proper to him and according to the analogy of participation, being, life and deification.[17]

Palamas thematizes the participability of God in terms of "energy." The question of the "energies" is basically the same problem that Plato faced. He saw the cosmos, not as a homogeneous continuum, but after the fashion of the primitive mentality that Mircea Eliade describes, as a series of levels that had to be bound together by some mediating principle. For example, Plato saw the universe as metaphysically divided into being and non-being. The mediator that bound these principles into a viable whole was "becoming."

Likewise, the world of ideas and that of sense were bound together in the soul of man. St. Gregory of Nyssa, in treating this problem in terms of the bridge between God and His creatures, was the first to use "energy" to describe the bond. St. Maximus used the term in a different sense altogether and made it equivalent to "real existence."[18]

Every "essence" has to have an "energy" if it is to be more than merely "possible." Gregory Palamas combined both meanings and applied the term to God's manifestations in the created order: God has real existence in the world insofar as He is manifested to the world. This is another way of saying: God has real existence in the world insofar as He *creates* the world, i.e., gives it existence by giving it a share in His own real existence in and through the *energies.*

## THE NATURE OF THE ENERGIES

The energies are manifestations of God. Still, even though

they are many and diverse, they are *one* in God. Hence, God's simplicity is maintained, but not at the price of isolating Him from contact with His creation. These manifestations are "God coming forth"—God insofar as He does not hide in His unknowable essence, but shows Himself to man.[19]

Archbishop Joseph Raya beautifully summarizes Palamas' doctrine in his book, *The Face of God:*

> It is not God's action but God himself in his action who makes himself known to man and gives him the ability to "see" him. God enters into man's love, remaining there in his intimate reality. The presence is real, indeed most real. This communication of God himself is called "Uncreated Energy." The uncreated energies of God are not 'things' which exist outside of God, not 'gifts' of God; they are God himself in his action. They are the very God who is himself Uncreated. They are therefore called 'uncreated' because their cause and origin is the Essence of God. In them God, as it were, goes beyond himself and becomes 'trans-radiant' in order to really communicate himself. Thus the Essence and energies of God are not 'parts' of God but two ways by which we human beings can contemplate God's essence.[20]

The energies are, we might say, "God *for us.*" They are God in loving and creative relationship to us out of the motive of sharing His holiness and inner life with us. Palamas introduces a distinction that is important in the history of the theology of God's knowability and unknowability. God for us is "Theos" whereas God in Himself is "Hyper-Theos."[21] We can see how again both the communicability and the incommunicability of God are preserved.

Palamas even speaks of the "two sides" of God: higher and lower, superior and inferior.[22] However, in thus distinguishing the two aspects of "God *in se*" and "God for us," Palamas is not introducing a dichotomy into God, as if there were "two Gods" (as Barlaam accused him of doing). Rather he is simply distinguishing the knowable from the unknowable in God.

## PARTICIPATION IN GOD'S ENERGIES

Palamas, as has been said above, works out a doctrine of God's essence and His uncreated energies in order to preserve the basic truth of Christian revelation, that man has been in God's eternal love act ordered to participate in His very own being. These eternal energies are the thoughts of God who is present in each of them. They are not, however, the essence of God. God is a living God who is at the same time transcendent in His essence but ever remains active in it through His energies.

For Eastern Christian thought, the energies signify an exterior manifestation of the Trinity. God is not determined by any of His attributes and all determinations are logically posterior to His essence. When God is described as love, life, truth, etc., we understand the energies as subsequent to the very being of the Trinity.

The doctrine of the energies, as distinct from the essence, is the basis of all mystical experience. God who is inaccessible in His essence is present in His energies "as a mirror," according to Palamas' saying, remaining invisible in that which He is. He is wholly unknowable in His essence, yet He is revealed in His energies.

This doctrine makes it possible to understand how the Trinity can remain incommunicable in essence, and yet dwell within us according to the promise of Christ. When one receives the deifying energies, one receives the indwelling of the Holy Trinity which is inseparable from its natural energies. The distinction made between the essence and energies makes it possible to preserve the real meaning of the words "partakers of the divine nature" (2 P 1:4). In deification, we are by grace what God is by nature, except that we remain creatures. St. Symeon the New Theologian (+1022) insists in writings that greatly influenced Palamas that we are made gods by participation, by grace.[23] The divine energies in themselves are not the relationship of God to created being, but they do enter into relationship with that which is not God and draw the world into existence by the will of God. The divine energies reveal the Divine Persons, but not the divine essence. Thus Palamas writes:

> You do not however consider that God lets Himself be seen in His superessential essence, but according to the deifying gift and according to His energy, according to the grace of adoption, uncreated deification and the direct hypostasized glory.[24]

The energies of God are uncreated divine activity. The divine essence, as has been said repeatedly above, is inaccessible. God, however, does communicate Himself. He can be known experimentally and we can reach Him in union or deification. Gregory Palamas' distinction between the essence of God which is unknowable and incommunicable and the energies or divine operations which are forces proper to and inseparable from God's essence in which He goes forth from Himself, manifests and communicates Himself, is a recognition of the fact that God is both totally inaccessible and at the same time accessible.

## PERSONALIZED ENERGIES

Thus for Palamas the divine energies are real (although not material nor merely an intellectual concept), essential (i.e., not an accident) and yet really distinct from the actual essence of the Godhead. In order to avoid introducing a "quaternity" of four Persons in God, Palamas insists on the energies being "enhypostaton," ( ἐνυπόστατον ) using the term introduced by Leontius of Byzantium in the 6th century as that which signifies what is possessed, used and manifested by a person.[25]

Here we come to the essential point of Palamas'

distinction between God's essence and His energies. He insists that the energy which the saints see, the φῶς ἐνυπόστατον, is essentially personalized, a common manifestation of the Three Persons of the Trinity. If this were not so, then God would be manifesting Himself and divinizing man through an extrinsic grace, an accident. The love relationship that allows God to share His very being and life with man would be only a moral arrangement and not a true regeneration of man into God's very own life. In a word, God would not be really giving Himself to man but He would be giving man a thing, different from His very own being, and man would be sanctified only in an extrinsic manner and not by direct contact with God's very own life.

But because the divine energy is essential and not an accident and personalized, *enhypostatized* or existing in its reality and manifestation completely in the three hypostases of the Trinity, we have the possibility of being united by God's grace to God and thus of becoming divine by participation (μετοχή) in this divine energy. We are not assimilated into the Absolute Universal Self in a Hindu non-duality sense, nor are we justified only extrinsically in Luther's sense without a completely new regeneration of our human nature. We are divinized through our participation in God's own essential energy, freely given as grace.

E. Hussey well summarizes this point:

> The saints clearly say that this adoption which has become a reality through faith, this deifying gift is enhypostasized. Barlaam alone considers the principle of deification and the deifying gift to be merely the imitation of God and he affirms that it is not enhypostasized; but this is quite different from the deification which the fathers knew and professed. The divine Maximus says that this deifying power is not only enhypostasized but also uncreated, but also beyond limits of space and time; and that those who possess it become thereby uncreated and beyond the limits of space and time, although in their own proper nature they are still creatures who have come from non-being.[26]

## GRACE

Palamas knows that the Greek language gives various meanings to the word *grace.* He writes:

> Sometimes it is the object given gratuitously which is called grace, but sometimes it is the very act of giving; at other times neither of these senses apply to the word 'grace,' which designates the beauty, the beautiful appearance, the ornament and the glory of each nature, and in this sense we speak of the grace of words and of conversation . . . Hence there is a grace of nature different from deifying grace.[27]

Palamas does not accept, therefore, the concept of a "created supernatural." He does accept the idea of a "created grace." Yet in this same work against Akindynos, Palamas shows that for him grace is primarily God communicating, giving, manifesting Himself to man.

> There is a created grace and another grace uncreated. . . but since the gift which the saints receive and by which they are deified is not other than God Himself, how can you say that this is a created grace?[28]

Man must open himself to God's uncreated energies that are always "gracing" man at every moment in each event. This is the mystery of the *synergy* that the Greek Fathers stress in their development of *praxis* or the ascetical life. Man may be tainted by sin and his fallen state inherited from his ancestors, yet he has freedom locked within his consciousness. He can rise and go back to his Father in a *metanoia,* in a conversion and surrender to God. When man cooperates, the result is a divine state produced within man's soul. "It is when you have in your soul the divine state that you really possess God within yourself; and the true divine state is love towards God, and it survives only by practice of the divine commandments."[29]

Man is divinized and reaches his fulfillment of being a child of God through the divine energies or grace. "God in His completeness deifies those who are worthy by uniting Himself with them, not through the hypostasis—that belonged to Christ alone—not through the essence, but through the uncreated energies."[30] Thus, although Palamas uses the term *grace* with the same flexibility and richness as did the other Greek Fathers, his primary definition of grace would probably be: God pouring Himself out to us by His divine energies in order that He might unite us with Him by making us true children of God. The primary meaning of grace (which admits of an infinity of growth) centers around God's energetic process of divinizing man into the very likeness of Jesus Christ, the image of the Father and yet the image according to whom we have all been created.

This process of purification and sanctification through which man grows in participating in the nature of the Divine admits of a continual growth unto infinity. The very nature of grace as God's life within man presupposes growth. To accept the divine energies as grace, therefore, is to accept the necessity of constantly moving toward God. St. Gregory of Nyssa had written: "The grace of the Holy Spirit is given to everyone with the understanding that there is to be an augmenting and increase of what is received."[31]

## DEIFICATION OF THE WHOLE MAN

One of Palamas' greatest contributions was to show that grace as the divinization process on the part of the Trinity towards man touches not merely man's soul or spirit. He cuts through the Platonizing tendency in Christian spirituality that interprets the Pauline categories of flesh and spirit as equivalents of the Platonic terms "matter" and "spirit" or "body" and "mind." Palamas reinstates them in their correct Biblical form as referring to man without Christ and man graced by the Holy Spirit, not as "material" and "immaterial." Thus "spiritual vision" does not mean mental vision, but rather participation of the whole man, body, soul, spirit, in the knowledge of God. Thus Palamas can write:

> The spiritual joy that comes from the spirit into the body is not at all broken by communion with the body, but transforms the body and makes it spiritual, for then it rejects all the evil appetites of the flesh, and does not drag the body down any more but rises up with it so that the whole man becomes "Spirit" according to what is written: "He who is born of the Spirit is Spirit" (Jn 3:6, 8)[32]

Palamas' holistic approach is refreshing in the light of Biblical research and modern theological approaches to an incarnational view of grace as God-for-man in all relationships, not merely God toward man-a-mind. Man is, therefore, for Gregory Palamas, made according to God's image and likeness precisely in his whole make-up, body, soul and spirit. In such a total openness on the part of man to God in His "graceful" energies on all levels of man's being, man fulfills the image and likeness as the crown of all of God's works, as the ruler of the cosmos.

Because man is opened to God's grace on all levels, including man's bodily relationships to God and cosmos, man is considered by Palamas as superior even to the angels.

> Whereas the angels are appointed to serve the Creator and have as their only mission to be under authority (it is not being given to them to rule over inferior beings unless they are sent to do this by the Preserver of all things), man is preordained not only to be ruled, but to rule over all that which is on the earth.[33]

Angels are endowed with a soul and a spirit, yet they are not joined to a body, Palamas insists, and hence are inferior to human beings who alone of all God's creatures can imitate "the passion and death of the Lord."[34]

Immortality, holiness and living according to the virtues of Jesus Christ constitute living proof of man's Godly-orientation. Man's progress in perfection as he consciously lives according to the image and likeness that is Jesus Christ is measured by his meaningful service to God, sharing God's freedom to do at all times the holy will of God.

## UNCREATED LIGHT

If God's grace operates also on the body-relationships, then the body also can experience repercussions of God's activities. This is precisely what Palamas insisted upon as he defended the ancient Eastern Christian form of mysticism called *Hesychasm* with its holistic approach to prayer, including the use of bodily postures and breathing techniques to aid the contemplative to meet the indwelling Trinity in the deification process.

*Hesychasm* is a form of Eastern Christian mysticism that has its roots in the spirituality of the Fathers of the Desert, especially that which developed from the Macarian school of the heart, as further developed on Mt. Sinai and in the 14th century on Mt. Athos.[35] It places great stress on ascetical practices and an interior attentiveness in controlling the movements of the "heart" so as to reach a state of inner tranquillity called *hesychia* (ἡσυχία) which in Greek means rest or tranquillity. With all of man's being, body, soul and spirit, integrated, he is able to be attentive to God's commands and wishes and is freed from unregulated "passions" to do always what most pleases God.

During the time of Palamas, Barlaam ridiculed the methods taught by the Hesychasts of breathing and bodily postures as an integral part of prayer. Barlaam gave them the colorful name of *omphalopsychoi* (literally, men-with-their-souls-in-their-navels). But the real issue was not a question of using techniques to pray but it was the pretention of the monks that in such deep, transcendental prayer they were claiming to "see God." We have pointed out Barlaam's form of nominalism and agnosticism that refused to accept any supernatural conception of knowledge of God. If it were any knowledge it would be natural intellection and this would yield only symbolic, not true, knowledge of God.

Gregory Palamas fought this approach with the conviction that the Kingdom of God was already present in the Church and that the present period of salvation, inaugurated by the Resurrection of Christ, was indeed the reign of Christ, a reign hidden under sacramental veils, but true and fully real for believers.

Christ always shone with the Trinitarian energy, the Thaboric Light, yet generally it remained invisible for most men. The Transfiguration was not a phenomenon limited in time and space. No change took place at that moment as far as Christ was concerned, not even in His human nature, but a change took place in the consciousness of the three Apostles who suddenly for some measure of limited time had the faculty of seeing the Master as He was, resplendent in eternal light. The Holy Spirit remains invisible to us, yet is constantly manifesting Himself in light through His sanctifying, deifying powers.

Is this light, that is uncreated, the operation of the whole Trinity in the divinization process of man into the image and likeness of God, also sensible and material? Is it merely intelligible? This light of illumination received in deep, mystical prayer, is beyond both intellect and senses, yet this light fills at once both man's intellect and senses. The *Tomus Hagioriticus*, a profession of faith, undoubtedly formulated chiefly by Palamas himself, but signed by other Orthodox bishops in 1340, distinguishes between a sensible light, a light of the intellect and finally the uncreated light, the prototype of these first lights and surpassing them both infinitely. The first two are effects, overflowing from the energizing light of the interior-dwelling Holy Spirit.

> When they (the ascetics) are worthy to receive this grace and supernatural power, they perceive both with the senses and with the intellect what is above all sense and all intellect in the way known only to God and those who have experienced this grace.[36]

Man becomes deified as he becomes filled with the Light of Thabor or of the Holy Spirit in the degree that he makes himself worthy of it by asceticism. Deification is not a one-sided act of God, but it is a cooperation between God and man, a *synergy.* The goal of the ascetical life is not to deaden the bodily passions, but rather to acquire a new energy which will allow both body and mind to share in the life of grace. According to the measure of his deification, man acquires knowledge of God (contemplation: *theoria* [ θεωρία ] in the Greek patristic sense) that is beyond every intellectual concept, a knowledge that is more a communion, a living experience between God and man.

As we have said above, the Fathers make the distinction between the knowable and unknowable in God that seems somehow to be overcome in the mystical union that is called "deification" by grace in which "man transcends his nature. Being mortal, he becomes immortal; being corruptible, he becomes incorruptible; having a short life, he receives life eternal; being man, he becomes God," as St. Gregory of Nyssa writes.[37]

Still, Palamus avoids Messalianism and Pelagianism that posited a state of divinization through man's own effort. Man, through God's free condescending love-act in Baptism, receives a new, divine life within himself. He is made by God's efforts or energies a totally different reality. It is what St. Paul calls a "new creature" (2 Co 5:17). Palamas, after the Christological controversies of Arianism, Nestorianism, Monophysitism and Monothelitism, stressed the impossibility of a created intermediary. This intermediary can only be the divine activity, the uncreated energy of God, conceived as grace. Grace can never, in its true and full sense, be considered by Palamas as a thing, a created gift. It is God working to effect with man's cooperation his divinization by participation.

Palamas, with his positive emphasis on the body as a vital part of the whole man, stresses that this divinizing grace also transforms the body, man's senses, his natural intellect, so that the entire, whole man participates even now in this life in the supreme act for which man was created: union with God. He summarizes this succinctly:

> The sensual and intellectual faculties constitute means of knowing beings. They are limited to beings and manifest the Divine through these beings. But those who possess not only powers of sensation and intellection, but have also attained spiritual and supernatural grace, are not limited by beings in their knowledge, but know also spiritually, above sense and intelligence, that God is Spirit, for in their entirety they become God, and they know God in God.[38]

It is Jesus Christ alone who has united divinity and humanity in His *hypostasis.* Thus He in His glorified human-divine life communicates to all baptized in His name the Divine Energy or Sanctifying Grace. For Palamas, there is no other grace worthy of the name; all else is natural. The glorified hypostasis of Christ becomes prolonged through His Church. Thus Christ becomes the divine and uncreated life of the individual Christian. The Church is a real, visible divinized community. One member living in Christ lives also with his fellow Christians in whom Christ also lives. Palamas asks: "For who shall divide those that are one, in accordance with the Master's prayer (Jn 17:21) and, united to the one God, by the one Word in the one Spirit?[39]

The Light of Thabor that certain mystics claimed to have experienced as a sign of growth in the divinization process does not have an existence of its own apart from the divinity it symbolizes, nor is it in any way a simple hallucination, according to Palamas. It is really a natural attribute of Christ's divinity that the three Apostles saw. Thus the mystic who can never see the essence of God as it really is can really see God in His energies. The Light of Thabor becomes for the hesychasts a natural symbol which Palamas describes as that which derives from the nature of the object of which it is a symbol. Heat, for example, is the symbol of the burning power of fire, or, in other words, its natural attribute.[40]

Thus Palamas insists upon a true knowledge of God in His energies: "He, who contemplates God not through the medium of a foreign symbol, but through a natural symbol, has seen God."[41]

## TRANSFIGURING LIGHT

In Palamas' use of the Thaboric Light as a symbol of the highest transforming power of the Trinitarian energies working on the whole man we can see his reliance on the writings of St. Symeon the New Theologian. Both Palamas and St. Symeon taught that such an immersion into the Trinitarian life admits of ecstatic moments in which God is seen as brilliant light within the darkness of man. The two areas, although separate, namely, God's ineffable beauty and glory and man's sinfulness that still needs healing, coexist in such an experience as we read in one of St. Symeon's hymns:

> But, O what intoxication of light, O what movements of fire!
> O, what swirlings of the flame in me, miserable one that I am,

coming from You and Your glory!
The glory I know it and I say it is Your Holy Spirit,
who has the same nature with You and the same honor,
O Word;
. . . I thank You that You have made me worthy to know,
however little it may be,
the power of Your divinity.
I thank You that You, even when I was sitting in darkness,
revealed Yourself to me, You enlightened me,
You granted me to see the light of Your countenance that
is unbearable to all.
. . . You appeared as light, illuminating me completely
from Your total light,
And I became light in the night, I who was found in the
midst of darkness.
Neither the darkness extinguished Your light completely,
nor did the light dissipate the visible darkness,
but they were together, yet completely separate,
without confusion, far from each other, surely,
not at all mixed.
. . . So I am in the light, yet I am found in the middle
of the darkness.
So I am in the darkness, yet still I am in the middle of
the light.[42]

For the Eastern Christian mystics there was a real vision of the Thaboric Light that occurred at various times, dependent upon one's growth in compunction and humility. But even when the vision of such a light was not present, the light-presence of the Trinity still shone in the strong, spiritual awareness of the indwelling Trinity. It is a contemplation that allows the intelligence to remain completely simple, totally integrated into God, stripped of all thoughts and bathed in the light of God. St. Symeon describes this inner light:

The intelligence cannot find any other object but the light on which it has been fixed. . . . It rests then in the abyss of the divine light which allows it to perceive nothing outside of itself. Indeed, this is what is meant: 'God is light'

> and the supreme light. For those who reach this, it is the repose of all contemplation.[43]

Such a light to the intellect is a prelude to the full glory that awaits the Christian totally transformed into Christ. This is what fills the Christian with perpetual happiness and drives out all passionate, disturbing thoughts and fills him with a vision, even now, that the Savior in the Sermon on the Mount promised when He said: "Blessed are the pure of heart, for they shall *see* God" (Mt 5:8). Man progressively becomes more transformed through the knowledge and contemplative experience of knowing God and of being known and loved by Him. This transformation is a form of the resurrection already enjoyed even to some degree in the body. Such a mystic-true theologian sees the Risen Lord Jesus as Mary Magdalen and the Apostles saw Him after His resurrection. Jesus Christ renders such a Christian, already through His Spirit, resurrected from the dead; He vivifies him and gives him Himself to see as completely living within him.

Such is the meaning of the ultimate stages of theology in which the contemplative, purified of all self-love, enters into a living relationship of continued communion with the Holy Trinity. He receives knowledge in the most *apophatic* sense: knowledge not by his own knowing, but knowledge infused by a mystical union of the indwelling Trinity. This is the meaning of Evagrius' statement that was so well understood by theologians who in that age were primarily mystics: "If you are a theologian you truly pray. If you truly pray you are a theologian."[44]

*CHAPTER FIVE*

# Theological Applications of Divine Energies

We have seen that the doctrine of the divine energies as developed by the Eastern Christian Fathers, especially in the synthesis given by St. Gregory Palamas, is a theological means of explicating the belief that God's being lies not only in incomprehensible Abolute Essence but also in immediate relations with His creation. Such a doctrine claims that God exists in two difference modalities: in His unapproachable essence and outside it in His energetic relationships to the created world. The energies signify an exterior manifestation of the Trinity.

The doctrine of the energies, as distinct from the essence, is the basis of all mystical experience. God who is inaccessible in His essence is present in His energies "as a mirror," according to the saying of Palamas, yet remaining invisible in that which He is. He is wholly unknowable in His essence, yet He is revealed in His energies.

This doctrine makes it possible to understand how the Trinity can remain incommunicable in essence and yet dwell within us according to the promise of Christ. If we might return now to Whitehead and perhaps also to Heidegger and draw some comparisons with the teaching of Palamas, I think the relevance of the uncreated energies for modern theology can be better seen.

Both Whitehead and the Greek Fathers, especially Palamas, would agree that the world is a dynamic rather than a static reality. If, for example, man in process-thought is a changing, developing creature, how much more true would this be for Palamas and the Greek Fathers in general, who see God transforming man into His likeness by His energies. A "process" approach to man is absolutely fundamental in the theology of the Fathers. We have seen Palamas' insistence that God, through His energies, is constantly transforming man so that He truly may become "a partaker in the divine nature."

Likewise with the world, as Whitehead would see the world in the process of change and growth, so would Palamas see the world being graced by the divine energies. God did not simply create and let the world go, but rather He continued to manifest His love through His energies.

Whitehead, as we have mentioned, sees the world as an inter-related society of "occasions." No man, for example, lives in isolation, but he is always projecting into the world new occasions. This is clearly at the heart of the "logos mysticism"[1] as taught by St. Maximus the Confessor (+622). For Maximus, as for St. John the Evangelist, the whole world is inter-related in its harmony according to the differentiated *logoi* or the created existence of individual things according to the mind of God. All things are created through the Logos through whom the creative will of the Father flows. St. Maximus presents us with a dynamic vision of a world united in the mind of God, of a world of ideal *logoi* in process of being attained as the existential *logoi* in creatures move to completion under the power of the *Logos,* Jesus Christ. Man, the center of the universe, possesses free will—the ability to live according to the *logos* in him, by fulfilling in union with

God's activity (energy-grace), this inner principle of harmony and order; or else man can reject it.

## THE MATERIAL WORLD AS SACRED

We have pointed out how Whitehead rejects all dualisms between mind and matter, natural and supernatural. Palamas and the Greek Fathers would be quite in accord with this type of thinking. For them, God is constantly gracing the world by His energies. If God is constantly operable in the world by His energies, then can we really speak of a distinction between the sacred and the profane as something really existing in the objective order? Is it not rather dependent upon the see-er, the contemplative who sees *inside* of the material world the loving and working presence of God, as one quite different from the non-contemplative who sees only the objective material world that presents itself to his senses?

The Greek Fathers would always be able to see the Creator working in His world and hence they would not be able to understand a time when the world would be seen purely as natural, lying outside of God's providential, loving activity. Certainly a distinction is made between Creator and creature, but from the beginning of creation the divine rays have penetrated the created universe.

We have pointed out how Whitehead rejects all dualisms between mind and matter, natural and supernatural. Palamas and the Greek Fathers would be quite in accord with this type of thinking. For them, God is constantly gracing the world by His energies. If God is constantly operable in the world by His energies, then can we really speak of a distinction between the sacred and the profane as something really existing in the objective order? Is it not rather dependent upon the see-er, the contemplative who sees *inside* of the material world the loving and working presence of God, as one quite different from the non-contemplative who sees only the objective material world that presents itself to his senses?

The Greek Fathers would always be able to see the Creator working in His world and hence they would not be able to understand a time when the world would be seen purely as natural, lying outside of God's providential, loving activity. Certainly a distinction is made between Creator and creature, but from the beginning of creation the divine rays have penetrated the created universe.

We have pointed out that the most important concern of Whitehead and those theologians who identify with his thinking is the way traditional theism presents God as not being really related to our life. Whitehead's answer to this dilemma is to posit a primordial and consequential nature to God. One cannot help but be struck by the similarity (but by no means identity) between this and Palamas' teaching on the essence and the energies of God. Both thinkers seem to want to retain a transcendent and an immanent dimension to God. Whitehead locates the transcendent in the primordial nature, while Palamas sees it in God's essence. As to the immanent aspect, Whitehead would locate this in the consequent nature of God, while Palamas would see this in the energies of God.

Secondly, Whitehead seems to depict God as somehow unfinished and incomplete. One is reminded of Hegel's concept of God as unfolding in the universe. I believe that Palamas' description of the energies of God allows us to see God as intimately related with His universe, and still we preserve the Christian belief in a Trinity as perfect and complete in itself.

The third corrective that Palamas can offer is a Trinitarian and Incarnational dimension which is lacking in Whitehead's thought. To be fair, Whitehead is speaking as a philosopher and not as a theologian. Nevertheless, if one is to be a Christian, one must place the Trinity and the Incarnation at the center of any discussion. If Whitehead possessed a

Trinitarian and Incarnational approach as did Palamas, then perhaps he would not have had the same degree of difficulty in seeing God as related to and involved in His creation.

## INSIGHTS FROM HEIDEGGER

Heidegger has a similar approach to God as a dynamic, energetic force always revealing Himself in the event of the moment in which truth is being discovered. For him *Being* is not in the generic categories of beings, nor is it "God," such as that word is generally understood in the West, namely, as the *ens realissimum* or *ens supremum*, nor is it even what the Medievals called *existentia.* Neither is it the sum total of the beings of the word considered in their generic unity of "beingness". *Being*, rather, for Heidegger is the *event of truth.* He analyzes the Greek word for truth and divides it into its two compartments: *a* (alpha privative, meaning *non-*) and -*lētheia* (meaning "hidden" or "concealed"). Truth, then, is the event of "non-concealment," or truth is "re-velation"—the removing of the veil so that *Being* may shine forth. In either case it is an *event* rather than a substance, an act of coming-forth (*evenire* in Latin).

Palamas makes a similar distinction between the *coming-forth* of God (πρόοδος) and the non-coming-forth (οὐκ πρόοδος) in order to distinguish the essence from the energies in God. If we agree that they are speaking of much the same thing, we can perhaps gain some insights concerning the question of participation in God.

Heidegger asserts that "The Holy . . . is only the essential space of Divinity,"[2] and "Only from the essence of the Holy can the essence of divinity be thought. Only in the light of the essence of divinity can it be thought and said what the word "God" is to signify."[3] These citations show that Heidegger distinguishes *divinity* from Godhead. St. Gregory of Nyssa made the same point that influenced Palamas when he wrote:

> The majority of people think that the word "Divinity" is properly applied to speaking about the divine nature. . . . But we follow the indications of the Bible and we know that this nature is unnamable and unspeakable; we say that every (divine) name whether it be invented by men or transmitted by the Scriptures, only serves to explain concepts relative to nature even when the meaning of nature is itself not understood. . . .[4]

Throughout his entire corpus, Heidegger likes to indicate that *Being hides* as it reveals beings. That is to say, it casts its light for the purpose of revealing beings and not immediately for the purpose of revealing itself. *Being* as truth serves as the *ground* of beings, but a ground that does not draw attention to itself. Rather, it thrusts beings out of itself. Let us tie together these two systems of thought, that of the Greek Fathers with their doctrine of divine energies and that of Heidegger.

Heidegger's ἀλήθεια (truth) is tantamount to Palamas' *energies.* The Christian truly participates in these energies. But the energies as ἀλήθεια hide as they reveal the beings of the world. To participate in the energies is to see the world from the viewpoint of God, which is to say, it is to love the world by a created participation in the uncreated and all-powerful love of God. Deification can be considered as a way of being more involved in the world than would be possible for one who does not accept the call of Christ.

Perhaps we could expand these statements a bit. The relation of the created order to God is an *ultimate* relation, that is, it is in the order of *existence (esse)* and not in the *ontic* order of concept of essence or the areas that correspond to concept or essence, namely, the inner-worldly realm of causality. Hence, to call God in to remedy a scene that is really the work of man is to fail to appreciate the *ultimate* nature of the world's relation to God. It is to ask God to take over man's work—and this, because of His love, He has chosen not to do. This would deprive man of his freedom, the only way he can grow ultimately into being a fulfilled loving child of God. This surely follows from the distinction that Palamas makes between primary and secondary causality in terms of the divine ideas.

Another insight that we can gain from this comparison deals with man's autonomy from God and flows from what was said above about love and freedom in man. If God has given man a share in His existence by participation in His energies, a share, it must be noted, that turns the world over to man as the realm of his power in the area of secondary causality, then we may speak of the metaphysical autonomy of the created order from God.

A *relative* autonomy this would be, to be sure, for to be a creature is *ipso facto* to be in relation—and yet in a certain sense it is to enjoy an inalienable autonomy—that is, one that God cannot withdraw from a necessity inherent in His own creative love.

If faith means to have the eschatological vision, and if the eschatological vision means, as Hans Urs von Balthazar has so often said, to see from the viewpoint of God, then what does the Christian see? From God's viewpoint, there is no God. To share in God's viewpoint is to be thrown into a situation where one never sees God as an object. St. John says as much. "No one has ever see God" (1 Jn 4:8). This is a salutary position with which to begin one's Christian commitment. Too often Christians, especially in the organs of official hierarchical admonition and teaching, give the impression that they indeed have seen God directly and are now standing in His position communicating truth to the world. St. John's position was somewhat less assuming, more *apophatic!*

After assuring us that no one of us has ever seen God, St. John goes on to write: "God is love and anyone who lives in love lives in God and God lives in him" (1 Jn 4:16). To be moving towards deeper human relationships means to be revealing more of God's loveliness to others in our relationships. This is not, according to our Christian faith, a mere extrinsicism that means we resemble somewhat what God would be like in human form. Our faith convinces us that it is actually God's very own life dynamically living in us and revealing His divinely loving presence within us outwardly toward others.

Experiencing God's energetic love in the love we have for others cannot happen unless Christians have first experienced God's energetic, personalized love within them in deep prayer, what the Greek Fathers called the *Prayer of the Heart.*[5] Such deep prayer allows the potential within the Christian to become a divinized child of God to burgeon forth into actualization. Such a person "knows" by a new consciousness, infused by the Holy Spirit of faith, hope and love, the abiding power of God, loving within him by His uncreated energies.

After assuring us that no one of us has ever seen God, St. John goes on to write: "God is love and anyone who lives in love lives in God and God lives in him" (1 Jn 4:16). To be moving towards deeper human relationships means to be revealing more of God's loveliness to others in our relationships. This is not, according to our Christian faith, a mere extrinsicism that means we resemble somewhat what God would be like in human form. Our faith convinces us that it is actually God's very own life dynamically living in us and revealing His divinely loving presence within us outwardly toward others.

Experiencing God's energetic love in the love we have for others cannot happen unless Christians have first experienced God's energetic, personalized love within them in deep prayer, what the Greek Fathers called the *Prayer of the Heart.*[5] Such deep prayer allows the potential within the Christian to become a divinized child of God to burgeon forth into actualization. Such a person "knows" by a new consciousness, infused by the Holy Spirit of faith, hope and love, the abiding power of God, loving within him by His uncreated energies.

In deep, interior prayer the love that thus emerges is not forced or contrived, although it is not easily achieved. One becomes aware of a deeper self emerging and surrenders the will in sacrifice and virtuous living in order that this true self might come to fullest development in God through a *synergy* of cooperation with the uncreated energies of the indwelling Trinity. Consequently one finds himself in true communion with both God and neighbor.

Such a *synergy* pushes the Christian outwardly into the contemporary world to become a "reconciler," as St. Paul frequently calls man, the new creature in Christ Jesus (2 Co 5:18). Thomas Merton puts it well when he writes: "It is only in assuming full responsibility for our world, for our lives and for ourselves that we can be said to live really for God."[6]

## ENERGIES AND GRACE

In the special theological areas of grace and divinization, which for the Greek Fathers were never separated, we can draw our final applications of the divine uncreated energies to modern theology. Vladimir Lossky, one of the most representative of modern Orthodox theologians who have evolved the theology of the Eastern Fathers to speak to the contemporary world, writes about the association of grace and the uncreated energies:

> In the tradition of the Eastern Church grace usually signifies all the abundance of the divine nature, insofar

> as it is communicated to men . . . the divine nature of which we partake through the uncreated energies.[7]

And in another place he writes; giving Palamas' clear distinction between energies and divine essence:

> Grace . . . is the energy or procession of the one nature: the divinity insofar as it is ineffably distinct from the essence and communicates itself to created beings, deifying them.[8]

John Meyendorff also describes grace in terms of the uncreated energies:

> The divine life—which is deifying grace when it is granted to man—therefore belongs to the divine nature even when men benefit from it (by grace and not by nature); hence it constitutes the means of a communion both personal and real with God, a communion which does not involve the impossible confusion of the natures.[9]

The West has suffered from the thought categories taken from Neo-Platonism by Augustine and inserted into Western theology and spirituality. But when Western schoolmen no longer were mystics like the earlier theologians who could discourse on contempolation and never separate it completely from God as Life, theology fell into a rationalization of man's anthropomorphic view of God. It forgot to view God from God's view as revealed in Holy Scripture and as commented on by the early Fathers in their view of salvific history through God's revealed Word.

Grace all too often became a "thing" to be amassed and stored up in some heavenly bank as security against the day of reckoning, instead of the Trinity living its uncreated energies within us, working dynamically to divinize us and through us to bring the Incarnation and Redemption to the world.

The greatest obstacle to spiritual progress was the conception of man's life, as Karl Rahner depicts it, as a two story building. On the first floor was man with a full human nature, all that came to him from God in creation, including the effects of the sin of the first man, Adam. Man acted purely as a human being on this leve, with the seeming implication that God was not too interested in this area except for the one faculty, man's will. This was the backstairs that led up to the second floor, the super-imposed supernatural life. Grace builds on nature and God gratuitously gives His gifts to a receiving human nature that is disposed to receive them. Thus an individual could live in two different compartments, at one time a purely "natural" life and again a "supernatural" life in the state of grace.

St. Thomas Aquinas, using Artistotle's categories, defines grace as the external principle of human actions. "Man needs a power added to his natural power by grace," wrote St. Thomas[10] This he calls grace, a thing which God bestows upon man. Habitual grace justifies the soul or makes it acceptable to God. It is the infused, God-assisted habit of doing what God approves. Actual grace is the supernatural reality which God gives as a means of assistance.

Some modern Roman Catholic theologians, such as Karl Rahner, warn against thinking of grace "materialistically." Grace, he says, is not a "created sanctifying 'quality' produced in a 'recipient' in a merely causal way by God."[11] Rahner comes very close to describing the uncreated energies as grace in terms similar to the Greek Fathers when he writes:

> Each one of the three divine persons communicates himself to man in gratuitous grace in his own personal particularity and diversity. This trinitarian communication is the ontological ground of man's life in grace and eventually of the direct vision of the divine persons in eternity.[12]

As long as grace is conceived of as solely a created entity, there cannot be an absolute mystery connected with it. If a created reality were substituted for God's self-communication, it would not be a communication of His Self. Rahner would conclude: "God would be the giver, not the *gift itself*."[13] The distinction of the Greek Fathers between the energies and the essence of God permits Eastern theologians to maintain the distinction between Giver and gift, while also claiming that God Himself is the gift. As Roland Zimany points out quite accurately:

> God, the essential Trinity, is the Giver, and God in His energies, which enable God to be known outside Himself and which are inseparable from the divine nature which they manifest, is the gift of uncreated grace.[14]

## DIVINIZATION

With the divine energies always surrounding man and lovingly calling him to respond to God's Word living within him and within the context of his existential life, man reaches his highest development in the continued cooperation *(synergy)* with God's energetic presence. When man continuously cooperates with God's grace as His divine uncreated energies manifested to man in the context of his daily life, he enters into the process of *theosis* or divinization which is the total integration of the body-soul-spirit relationships of man with God. This is the end of God's creation of man as His masterpiece. St. Irenaeus well expresses the divinization process as a development of the image and likeness of God in man:

> By their continuing in being throughout a long course of ages, they (men) shall receive a faculty of the Uncreated, through the gratuitious bestowal of eternal existence upon them by God. . . But being in subjection to God is continuance in immortality and immortality is the glory of the Uncreated One. By this arrangement, therefore, and these harmonies and a sequence of this nature, man, a

> created and organized being, is rendered after the image and likeness of the Uncreated God.[15]

The divinization process makes us united with God in His energies through a union by grace. We are made participators in the divine nature without, however, changing our human nature into the divine. St. Symeon the New Theologian puts the stress on the "awareness" on the part of the Christian of this process of regeneration. Over and over in his writings, he insists that the grace of the Holy Spirit regenerates us, making us gods by adoption, sons of God by "disposition and grace." He writes:

> . . . the adoption through regeneration is due to the Holy Spirit who makes us become gods by disposition and grace *(thesei kai chariti)* who makes us called heirs of God and co-heirs with Christ . . . whereby we see God and Christ Himself living in us according to His divinity and moving around in a conscious *(gnostos)* manner within us.[16]

A contribution of the Eastern concept of divinization to Western theology is both in the holistic influence of grace divinizing the whole person, body, soul and spirit, and in the dynamics of a growth process coming out of man's observation of God's commandments in the existential situation in which he finds himself. The Eastern approach has God not only divinizing man in his totality, but through man's cooperation God is effecting the "spiritualization" of the entire cosmos, bringing it into the resurrectional influence of Jesus Christ, who with man's cooperation is bringing all things into fullness (Col 1:20). This places the end for all people, not merely those who religiously follow both the "precepts" and the "counsels," to grow infinitely into a more God-like, ontological relationship, into a new creation. The West can profit from the Eastern theology of growth into the image and likeness of God since it is developed within the history of concrete salvation, beginning with God's initial creation, man's free rejection of this divinization through sin, the restoration of this primitive filiation with God through the Divine Son made man, the ever progressing movement of sanctification through the Holy Spirit working in the human being's life to refashion it in the imitation of Christ, giving us an ontological dynamism that is verified in Scripture and in the spiritual life of each individual.

## PROFIT FOR EASTERN THEOLOGY

We cannot be blinded to the fact that in the Eastern synthesis there are lacunae and deficiences. Through the use of metaphors such as image, likeness, model, mirror, sun and light rays, this whole doctrine, designed to explain the relation of God with finite man, the inter-relation of nature and grace, can be relegated to a lack of precision in speech and concept that leaves us with mere verbalism or at best beautiful poetry.

The theology of the Eastern Fathers is bound intimately with their doctrine of the spiritual and mystical life. Theology is the science about God and the spitirual life in the concrete striving towards God as man's ultimate goal. Perhaps from a deeper study of patristic theology, especially anthropology as seen by the Greek Fathers in the intimate relationship to the spiritual life, Western theology can regain something of its existential dynamism, and theology will become again a *life in God.* The Eastern theology can profit by being complemented in this doctrine of the uncreated energies and the image and likeness by the teachings of St. Augustine and St. Thomas.[17] Both of these theologians of the West have used also the model of image and likeness in working out a theological anthropology. Through much debating under the attacks of various heresies against grace, they were able to fashion concepts capable of clearly distinguishing the various points of relationship between nature in its different historical and possible stages and grace while all the time preserving God's gratuitous gift of grace and man's freedom to accept and to cooperate.

The Eastern tradition, with its fresh insight into the central truth of the Christian message that God condescends in His acitivities, especially through the God-Man, Jesus Christ, to make us into new creatures, "participators in the divine nature" (2 P 1:4), can keep before the Western mind, so gifted in logical thinking, this unique ontological relationship between God and man. Man's whole nature is to become, through God's energies of grace working on him, a living image of his Creator.

The words of St. Gregory of Nyssa form a fitting close to this work. They speak the reverent mind of all the early Eastern Fathers as they contemplate what it means that God should so love man as to create him according to His image and likeness and surround him constantly with His loving energetic activities that are destined to divinize man into a *real* child of God, if man consents to live according to his dignity:

> Man who among beings counts for nothing, who is dust, grass, vanity, who was adopted to be a son of the God of the universe, becomes the friend of this Being of such excellence and grandeur; this is a *mystery* that we can neither see nor understand nor comprehend. What thanks should man give for so great a favor? What word, what thought, what lifting up of mind in order to exalt the superabundance of this grace? Man surpasses his own very nature. From a mortal being he becomes immortal, from a perishable being he becomes imperishable. From ephemeral he becomes eternal. In a word, from man he becomes god. In fact, rendered worthy to become a son of God, he will have in himself the dignity of the Father, enriched by all the inheritance of the goods of the Father. O munificence of the Lord, so bountiful. . . . How great are the gifts of such ineffable treasures![18]

# Notes

## INTRODUCTION

1. Karl Jaspers: *The Origin and Goal of History* (New Haven: Yale University Press, 1953) p. 140.
2. Wm. M. Thompson: *Christ and Consciousness* (New York: Paulist Press, 1977) p. 183.

## CHAPTER ONE

1. Gerard Manley Hopkins: *God's Grandeur.*
2. St. Irenaeus: *Adversus Haereses:* Bk. V, ch. 28,4, *ANF (The Ante-Nicene Fathers* Vol. 1, ed. A. Roberts and J. Donaldson (Grand Rapids: Eerdmans, 1958) p. 557.
3. St. Thomas: *Summa Theologiae,* 1a 2ae, Q.109, intro., 2 ans.Q.110,1 ans.
4. St. Augustine: *De Trinitate,* Bk. 5,8-9.
5. cf.: John Chethimattam, C.M.I., *Consciousness and Reality* (Bangalore: Bangalore Press, 1967) pp. 233-40; also: Ewert Cousins: "Trinity and World Religions," in: *Journal of Ecumenical Studies,* Vol. 7, no. 3 (1970) pp. 476-498.
6. St. Bonaventure: *Quaestiones Disputatae de Mysterio Trinitatis,* 1 sent., d.3, p.1, a.un., q.4.

7. St. Gregory Palamas: *Capita Physica*, 68, *PG* 150, 1169.

8. cf.: G. Maloney, S.J.: The Cosmic Christ from Paul to Teilhard (N.Y.: Sheed & Ward, 1968); R. Hale: *Christ and the Universe. Teilhard de Chardin and the Cosmos* (Chicago: Franciscan Press, 1973).

9. M. Schmaus: *Katolische Dogmatik* (München; 1963) 11, 2, p. 461.

10. St. Maximus the Confessor: *Quaestiones ad Thalassium*, 21; PG 90, 312-316.

11. St. Maximus the Confessor:*Epistola XXI;* PG 91,604 BC.

12. St. Athanasius: *De Incarnatione Verbi;* PG 25,192B.

13. St. Cyril of Alexandria: *De recta Fide ad Theodosium;* PG 76,1177 A.

14. S. Bulgakov: *Paraclet* (Paris, 1946) pp. 268, 270.

15. P. Evdokimov: "L'Esprit Saint et l'Eglise d'après la tradition liturgique," in: *L'Esprit Saint et l'Eglise.* Actes du Symposium organisé par l'Académie Internationale des Sciences Religieuses (Paris, 1969) p. 92.

16. S. Bulgakov, op. cit., pp. 145, 164, 174 f.

17. Thomas Hopko: "Holy Spirit in Orthodox Theology and Life," in: *Commonweal* (Nov. 8, 1968), Vol. LXXXIX, no. 6, p. 187.

18. Teilhard de Chardin: "Super-Humanité, Super-Christ, Super-Charité," in: *Oeuvres de Pierre Teilhard de Chardin:* Vol. 9: Science et Christ (Paris: Editions du Seuil, 1965) p. 213.

19. For further development of this theme, cf.: G. Maloney: *Inscape: God at the Heart of Matter* (Denville, N.J.: Dimension Bks., 1978).

20. Julian of Norwich: *Showings;* tr. E. Colledge and J. Walsh, in: *The Classics of Western Spirituality* (N.Y.—Ramsey, N.J.: Paulist Press, 1978) p. 183.

21. R.A. Errico: *The Lord's Prayer* (San Antonio: Aramaic Bible Center, Inc., 1975) p. 13.

22. Louis de Blois, quoted by H.A. Reinhold: *The Soul Afire* (Garden City, N.Y.: Image Bks. Doubleday & Co., 1973) p. 358-359.

23. Teilhard de Chardin: *Le Milieu Mystique*, as found in Pensée 80, in: *Hymn of the Universe* (N.Y.: Harper Torchbooks, 1965) p. 154.

## CHAPTER TWO

1. St. Thomas Aquinas: *Super Epistolas S. Pauli*, ed. P. Raphaelis Cal, O.P. (Rome: Marietti, 1953) pp. 22-23.
2. Louis Dupré: "Transcendence and Immanence as Theological Categories," *Proceedings of the Thirty-First Annual Convention of the Catholic Theological Society of America* 31 (1976) pp. 1-10.
3. Cf.: John Arakkal: "The Dialectics of Belief and Life: the Need for a New Orientation in Theology," *Jeevadhara* (Nannamam, Kerala, 1976) no. 31, pp. 34-110.
4. For some key books on this topic cf.: A. N. Whitehead: *Process and Reality* (New York: Macmillan, 1969); Schubert Ogden: *The Reality of God* (New York: Harper & Row, 1966); Norman Pittenger: *Process Thought and Christian Faith* (New York: Macmillan, 1968); Daniel Day Williams: *The Spirit and the Forms of Love* (New York: Harper & Row, 1968).
5. Williams, p. 107.
6. Pittenger, p. 12.
7. Ibid., p. 13.
8. Whitehead, p. 520.
9. Ogden, p. 48.
10. Ibid., p. 51.
11. Williiams, p. 109.
12. Cf.: Henri de Lubac, S.J.: *Le surnaturel: Études historiques* (Paris: Aubier, 1946), p. 493.
13. On the doctrine of the image and likeness of God in man, cf.: G. Maloney, S.J., *Man: The Divine Icon* (Pecos, N.M.: Dove Pulications, 1973).
14. *Imitation of Christ*, Book III, Ch. 54-55.
15. St. Irenaeus: *Adversus Haereses*, IV, 64; *PG* 7.
16. Ibid., III, 19, 1 (citation from *The Ante-Nicene Fathers*, Vol. I, pp. 448-449).

## CHAPTER THREE

1. Thomas Merton gives this detail of Barth's life. Cf.: *Conjectures of a Guilty Bystander* (Garden City: Doubleday, 1966) p. 3.
2. St. Hilary of Poitiers: *The Trinity*, tr. by Stephen McKenna, C.SS.R., in *The Fathers of the Church* (N.Y., 1954) Vol. 25, p. 36.
3. Pseudo-Dionysius: *The Mystical Theology* in: *Mysticism: A Study and Anthology*, ed. by F. C. Happold (Baltimore: Penguin, 1971) pp. 215-216.
4. On this approach to apophatic theology consult the essay by Cyprian Kern: "Les elements de la théologie de Grégorie Palamas," in *Irénikon* 20 (1947) pp. 6-33.
5. Ibid., p. 9.
6. V. Lossky: *Vision of God* (Clayton, Wisc.: Faith Press, 1963) pp. 71, 74.
7. St. Gregory of Nyssa: *Comm. on Canticle of Canticles; PG* 44, 1001B.
8. St. Gregory of Nyssa: *Contra Eunomium*, XII; *PG* 45, 940D.
9. Ibid., 941B.
10. *Comm. on Cant. of Canticles; PG* 44, 939D.
11. *Comm. on Ecclesiastes*, sermon 7; *PG* 44, 729D-732A.
12. *Comm. on Cant. of Canticles; PG* 44, 1000D.
13. Cf.: L. Bouyer: *The Spirituality of the New Testament and the Fathers* (N.Y.: Désclée, 1960) p. 356.
14. St. Gregory of Nyssa: *On Perfection*, tr. by Virginia Woods Callahan in *Ascetical Works of Gregory of Nyssa;* in: *The Fathers of the Church*, Vol. 58, p. 122.
15. St. Gregory of Nyssa: *The Life of Moses; PG* 44, 397D-405A.
16. *Comm. on Cant. of Canticles; PG* 44, 1031B.
17. *Life of Moses; PG* 44, 405 A-D.
18. *Ibid.*, 397D-405A.
19. For the complete text in English see: F. C. Happold: *Mysticism*, cf. n. 3.

20. V. Lossky: *The Mystical Theology of the Eastern Church* (London: James Clarke & Co., 1957) p. 43.
21. *Mystical Theology*, p. 214.
22. The feast of the Epiphany, Matins, Canon 9.
23. *Grégoire Palamas—Les Triads pour la defense des saints Hesychastes*, 3 vols., ed. by John Meyendorff (Louvain: Spicilegium Sacrum Lovaniense, 1959) Triad, II, 3, 67.
24. Ibid., II, 3, 33.
25. Cf. John Meyendorff: *A Study of Gregory Palamas;* tr. George Lawrence (London: Faith Press, 1964) p. 132.
26. *Triads*, II, 3, 26.
27. Meyendorff, p. 131.
28. Basil Krivoshein: "The Ascetical and Theological Teaching of Gregory Palamas," in: *The Eastern Churches Quarterly* 3 (1938-1939) p. 72.
29. Lossky: *Mystical Theology of the Eastern Church*, p. 116.
30. Krivoshein, p. 145.

## CHAPTER FOUR

1. Cf.: G. Maloney, S.J.: *Man—The Divine Icon*, pp. 15-20.
2. See Roland D. Zimany: "The Divine Energies in Orthodox Theology," in: *Diakonia* 2 (1976) pp. 281-285.
3. St. Basil: *Epistle to Eustathius*, quoted by George Habra: "The Patristic Sources of the Doctrine of Gregory Palamas on the Divine Energies," in: *Eastern Churches Quarterly* 12 (1957-1958) p. 298.
4. Basil: *Epistle to Amphilochius*, cited by G. Habra, ibid., p. 300.
5. Ibid., p. 299.
6. Ibid., p. 296.
7. Ibid., St. Gregory of Nyssa: *Against Eunomius*, XII, p. 300.
8. *Celestial Hierarchy*, 1.
9. *Divine Names*, 1.
10. *Mystical Theology*, 1.

11. *Divine Names,* 11.

12. *Celestial Hierarchy,* 1.

13. *Mystical Theology,* 1, Happold, p. 212.

14. *Divine Names,* 2.

15. Ibid., 1.

16. Meyendorff: *A Study of Gregory Palamas,* p. 210.

17. *Triads,* III, 2, 24.

18. Johy Meyendorff: *St. Grégoire Palamas et la mystique orthodoxe* (Paris: Éditions du Seuil, 1959) p. 47.

19. Meyendorff: *A Study of G. Palamas,* p. 221-222.

20. Archbishop Joseph Raya: *The Face of God* (Denville, N.J.: Dimension Books, 1976) pp. 37-38.

21. Meyendorff: *Study,* p. 218, n. 63.

22. Krivoshein, p. 15.

23. See G. Maloney, S.J.: *The Mystic of Fire and Light: St. Symeon the New Theologian* (Denville, N.J.: Dimension Books, 1975) pp. 71-72.

24. *Triads* III, 1, 29.

25. M. Edmund Hussey: "The Persons—Energy Structure in the Theology of St. Gregory Palamas," in: *St. Vladimir's Theological Quarterly* 18 (1974) p. 3.

26. Ibid., p. 5.

27. Palamas: *Against Akindynos,* II, 9.

28. Ibid., III, 8.

29. *Triads,* II, 3, 77.

30. *Against Akindynos,* V, 26.

31. St. Gregory of Nyssa: *Christian Mode of Life,* in: *The Fathers of the Church,* vol. 58, p. 130.

32. *Triads* II, 2, 9.

33. Krivoshein, p. 28.

34. Ibid.

35. On the subject of hesychasm, cf.: G. A. Maloney, S.J.: *Russian Hesychasm* (The Hague: Mouton, 1973) and John Meyendorff: *St. Gregory Palamas and Orthodox Spirituality* (New York: St. Vladimir's Seminary Press, 1974).

36. *Tomus Hagioriticus; PG* 150, 1233.

37. St. Gregory of Nyssa: *On the Beatitudes,* 7; *PG* 44, 1280C. On St. Gregory's doctrine of the divine nature and the distinctions in God, cf.: Archbishop Basil Krivoshein: "Simplicity of the Divine Nature and the Distinctions in God, according to St. Gregory of Nyssa," in: *St. Vladimir's Theological Quarterly,* 21 (1977) pp. 76-104.

38. *Triads* II, 3, 68.

39. Homily 53, ed. S. Oikonomos (Athens, 1861) p. 180.

40. *Triads* III, 1, 13-14.

41. Ibid., 1, 35.

42. *Hymns of Divine Love by St. Symeon the New Theologian,* tr. by G. A. Maloney, S.J. (Denville, N.J.: Dimension Books, 1975) Hymn 25, pp. 135-36.

43. *St. Symeon the New Theologian: Chapitres théologiques, gnostiques et pratiques;* Vol. 51, in: *Sources Chrétiennes* (Paris: Cerf, 1968) 2, 17. For more development of this subject see: G. Maloney, S.J.: *The Mystic of Fire and Light: St. Symeon the New Theologian* (Denville, N.J.: Dimension Books, 1975).

44. Evagrius Ponticus: Praktikos: Chapters on Prayer; ed. John Eudes Bamberger, O.C.S.O. (Spencer, Mass.: Cistercian Publications, 1970) no. 60, p. 65.

## CHAPTER FIVE

1. For a development of this doctrine see the two writings of G. Maloney, S.J.: *The Breath of the Mystic* (Denville, N.J.: Dimension Books, 1974) pp. 141-160 and *The Cosmic Christ: From Paul to Teilhard* (New York: Sheed & Ward, 1968) pp. 167-178.

2. "Letter on Humanism," found in Heidegger's: *Plato's Doctrine of Truth,* tr. John Barlow, in: *Philosophy in the Twentieth Century,* ed. Wm. Barrett and H. D. Aiken (New York: Random House, 1962) pp. 286 ff.

3. Ibid., p. 294.

4. St. Gregory of Nyssa: *To Ablabius; PG* 45, 120D-121D.

5. On the Prayer of the Heart, cf.: G. A. Maloney, S.J.: *Inward Stillness* (Denville, N.J.: Dimension Books, 1976).

6. Thomas Merton: *Contemplation in a World of Action* (Garden City, N.Y.: Doubleday, 1971) p. 54.
7. V. Lossky: *Mystical Theology*, pp. 162-163.
8. Ibid., p. 172.
9. J. Meyendorff: *A Study of Gregory Palamas*, p. 217.
10. St. Thomas: *Summa Theologiae*, 1a 2ae, Q. 109, intro., 2 ans. Q. 110, 1 ans.
11. K. Rahner: *The Trinity*, tr. Joseph Donceel (New York: Herder & Herder, 1970) p. 23.
12. K. Rahner: *Nature and Grace*, tr. Dinah Wharton (London: Sheed & Ward), 1963) p. 24.
13. Rahner: *Trinity*, p. 101.
14. Roland D. Zimany: "Grace, Deification and Sanctification: East-West," in: *Diakonia* 12 (1977) p. 125.
15. St. Irenaeus: *Adversus Haereses* IV, 39, 2-3, in: *The Ante-Nicene Fathers*, Vol. 1, pp. 522-523.
16. St. Symeon: *Catacheses*, 24; cited by G. Maloney: *Mystic of Fire and Light*, p. 72.
17. Cf.: P. Camelot, O.P.: "La théologie de l'Image de Dieu," in: *Revue des Sciences Phil. et Théol.*, 1956, pp. 470-471.
18. Gregory of Nyssa: *De Beatitudine*, Or. VII; *PG* 44, 1280 B-C.